200

ONE POT MEALS

JOANNA FARROW

An Hachette UK Company
www.hachette.co.uk

First published in Great Britain in 2008 by Hamlyn,
a division of Octopus Publishing Group Ltd,
Carmelite House, 50 Victoria Embankment,
London EC4Y 0DZ
www.octopusbooks.co.uk

This edition published in 2016

ISBN 978-0-600-63339-6

A CIP catalogue record for this book is available from the
British Library

Printed and bound in China

10 9 8 7 6 5 4 3 2 1

Standard level spoon measurement are used in all recipes.
1 tablespoon = one 15 ml spoon
1 teaspoon = o   5 ml spoon

Both imperial a
recipes. Use o
of both.

Eggs should b
Department of
consumed raw
lightly cooked
such as pregn
babies and yo
dishes made v
kept refrigerate

Ovens should
if using a fan-a
instructions fo

This book incl
It is advisable
nuts and nut c

vulnerable to these allergies, such as pregnant and nursing
mothers, invalids, the elderly, babies and children, to avoid
dishes made with nuts and nut oils. It is also prudent to check
the labels of pre-prepared ingredients for the possible inclusion
of nut derivatives.

contents

introduction

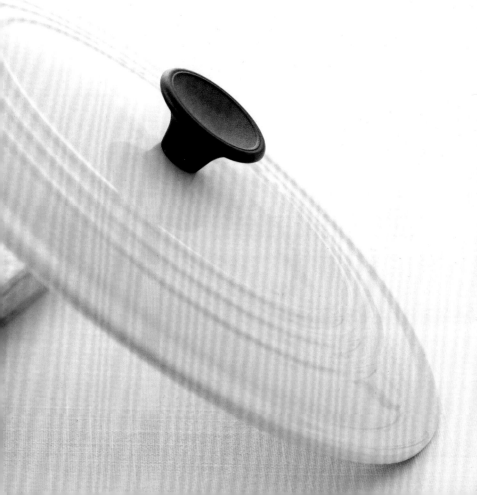

introduction

Some of the most delicious dishes imaginable are cooked in one pot, from comforting, warming stews and casseroles to intensely flavoured pot roasts and bakes. Most one pot dishes are cooked slowly and gently, ensuring that the ingredients are meltingly tender and bathed in flavour-packed sauces and gravies. Not only is the cook's job made simple, with just a little frying off required before adding various other ingredients, but recipes can be made ahead and left to simmer away on the hob or in the oven, leaving far less washing up than a meal of many different components. In most cases, their cooking times are very flexible and a one pot dish won't spoil if left a little longer in the oven than anticipated.

Equipment

Successful one pot cooking depends largely on the use of good-quality utensils. The recipes in this book use a range of pots, pans and baking dishes. The sturdier these are, the longer they will last and the more rewarding and easy they will be to use.

Flameproof casseroles

These are the most useful of all the one pot utensils, as you can start cooking on the hob, for example frying off onions and searing meat, before adding other ingredients and transferring the casserole to the oven for slow cooking to give tender, succulent results. This is particularly useful if you want to prepare a recipe and leave it to cook safely while you get on with other things.

Enamelled, cast-iron casserole dishes with ovenproof handles are available in various sizes, as are sturdy, heavy-based saucepans with ovenproof double handles for an easy grip. If you don't have any pans that can be used both on the hob and in the oven, use a frying pan and tip the fried ingredients into a casserole dish to finish cooking.

Saucepans

Saucepans are available in various different types of metals. Good-quality, heavy-based pans are a sound investment and won't buckle or burn during cooking. Efficient heat conduction means you can leave them on the back burner without the risk of ingredients catching on the base. Robust, nonstick pans are also a wise choice, being easy to use and to wash up. Avoid cleaning them in the dishwasher (even if they're dishwasher proof), as they're more likely to discolour and fade.

Sauté pans

These wide, shallow pans are deeper than frying pans and useful for recipes where you're gently frying meat or fish before

adding stock, wine or other liquids. A large frying pan makes a good substitute as long as it is deep-sided so that the contents can be stirred without slopping over the sides.

Frying pans

Several of the recipes in this book are cooked in a large, heavy-based frying pan, which enables you to fry off ingredients successfully (see page 10) and incorporate plenty of other ingredients. Some are available with lids, but you can use foil secured around the rim instead.

Woks

Woks are great for simmering, steaming and deep-frying as well as stir-frying. Their rounded base is designed to encourage the heat to encircle the whole pan and cook quickly and evenly. They're also great for recipes where your regular frying pan is not quite large enough to incorporate all the ingredients. Choose a completely round-based wok for a gas hob or one with a slightly flattened base for an electric hob. Woks vary considerably in quality and it's worth investing in a good one.

Baking dishes

Where a one pot recipe is assembled in a dish, without the need to fry off any ingredients first, a shallow baking dish that can be taken directly to the table is very useful in the kitchen.

Roasting pans

Roasting pans have to endure very high temperatures, both in the oven and on the hob, so a good-quality one that doesn't buckle or catch is essential. As some of the recipes require a large pan so that the ingredients have space to caramelize rather than steam, choose the largest one that will fit comfortably in your oven. Many deep-sided roasting pans are fitted with handles. This makes lifting them out of the oven safer.

Basic techniques

Frying off ingredients, particularly meat and poultry, is one the most crucial elements of successful one pot cooking. The process both develops a good flavour and adds a rich colour to stews, casseroles and pot roasts. In many recipes, butter is combined with oil for frying off. This ensures plenty of flavour from the butter, while the oil prevents the butter from burning.

Make sure the meat is thoroughly dry first, if necessary pressing it between several sheets of kitchen paper, then season and flour the pieces, if recommended. Heat the fat in the flameproof casserole or frying pan and add some of the meat, spreading the pieces so that each has space around it. Don't add too many pieces at once or the meat will steam in its own juice. Fry the pieces, shaking the pan gently, but without turning them, until deep brown on the underside. Using a wooden spatula, turn the pieces until browned all over, then drain with a slotted spoon while you fry the next batch.

Sometimes whole pieces of meat or poultry are seared in a pan before pot roasting. Use the same process, slowly turning the joint in the fat, not forgetting to sear the ends as well.

Ingredients

A few basic ingredients crop up frequently in one pot recipes. Keeping your storecupboard topped up with a selection of oils, herbs, spices, sauces and condiments provides plenty of variety in flavour. Check storage advice; some need refrigeration once opened.

Herbs

Herbs are one of the most appetizing ingredients to add to any dish and can be used liberally, their fragrant, aromatic flavours mingling with and complementing almost any meat, fish or vegetarian dish. Hardier herbs such as bay, thyme and rosemary are usually added to a dish early on in the cooking process, while more delicate herbs such as basil, coriander, dill and tarragon are stirred in towards the end.

Frozen herbs are a useful standby, particularly delicate ones such as chives, tarragon, fennel and dill. If you've bought too many fresh ones or have a glut from the garden, chop them and freeze them in little freezer bags for later use. Dried herbs are a less desirable substitute, with the exception of oregano, which is often used in rich tomato sauces. Dried herbs also deteriorate fairly quickly, dulling in colour and developing a musty aroma.

Oils

Most of the recipes use olive oil for frying and it is particularly appropriate for Mediterranean dishes. Olive oils range from light and mild to extra-virgin and all can be used for frying – though you might not want to use your most expensive extra-virgin oil, which is best kept for dressings. Some olive oils are infused with flavours such as basil, garlic and chilli. These are also good for frying, though chilli oil is best used sparingly, as some brands are very hot. Where a recipe doesn't specify a particular oil, you can use a vegetable oil such as sunflower, corn or groundnut oil. A few of the Asian dishes require 'stir-fry' or 'wok' oil. These are seasoned with flavours such as garlic and ginger, though you can use an ordinary vegetable oil instead.

Pesto

There are several different types of pesto now stocked alongside the traditional Italian green pesto of basil, pine nuts, olive oil, garlic and Parmesan. Red pesto, made with sun-dried tomatoes, is as widely used, and other

flavours such as fennel, aubergine and walnut are available. A spoonful of pesto can be used to liven up a 'thin' sauce, or form the base of the easiest one pot meal of all – tossed with pasta for a speedy supper.

Spices

A good supply of spices adds plenty of variety to one pot cooking, but, like dried herbs, they deteriorate over time. Check any you've had in store for a while, and if they've lost their spicy aroma, throw them away.

For most recipes it's best to buy whole seeds such as cumin, coriander, fennel and cardamom and grind them yourself using a pestle and mortar. A small bowl and the end of a rolling pin make a useful substitute.

Stock

A good-quality, flavour-packed stock is essential to so many one pot dishes, whether fish, meat, poultry or vegetable. There are now some good-quality powdered stocks, which make great storecupboard standbys, as well as liquid concentrates and bought ready-made stocks. Some of these are vacuum-packed and don't need refrigeration, while those from the chiller cabinets will last several days. However, the best option is to make your own when fresh or cooked bones are available. It takes just a few minutes to get the stock pot going – the rest takes care of itself. Once made, all cooled, strained stocks can be frozen in airtight containers or freezer bags for three to six months.

Tomato purée

A storecupboard essential, tomato purée is an intense tomato concentrate that adds flavour and colour to various dishes. Sun-dried tomato paste has a sweeter flavour and is perfect for Mediterranean dishes.

Accompaniments

The term 'one pot' implies that there are no other pots and pans used in a recipe. This can be the case with all the recipes in this book, unless, of course, you're hankering for a portion of creamy mash or buttery greens to serve with a comforting stew or casserole. For convenience, and to satisfy hungry appetites, a well-flavoured bread, warmed through shortly before the dish is ready, is the most effortless accompaniment to one pot dining. A mixed or leafy herb salad is another easy accompaniment.

Ready-cooked rice and noodles make useful storecupboard staples and are easy to reheat following the packet instructions, or they can be stirred into a dish before serving. A bag of couscous is also worth keeping in store and is very easy to prepare. For four servings, tip 250 g (8 oz) couscous into a heatproof bowl 10 minutes before the one pot dish is ready to serve. Add 300 ml (½ pint) boiling water or stock, cover and leave to stand until the couscous absorbs the water – about 10 minutes. Fluff up with a fork and season to taste, adding extra flavours such as finely grated lemon rind, toasted nuts, saffron threads, chopped herbs or flavoured oils. Use the same method for bulgar wheat, but allow about 20 minutes for the water or stock to be absorbed. Some of the recipes include a seperate accompaniment recipe. These are tasty suggestions, and not essential.

poultry & game

thai chicken pot roast

Serves **3–4**
Preparation time **15 minutes**
Cooking time **1 hour
35 minutes**

1.25 kg (2½ lb) **chicken**
1 tablespoon **Thai seven-
spice seasoning**
2 tablespoons **oil**
3 **garlic cloves**, crushed
1 **hot red chilli**, deseeded
and sliced
40 g (1½ oz) **fresh root
ginger**, finely chopped
200 ml (7 fl oz) **chicken stock**
2 **lemon grass stalks**,
chopped
1 tablespoon **fish sauce**
1 tablespoon **caster sugar**
2 tablespoons **lime juice**
50 g (2 oz) **fresh coriander**,
plus extra to sprinkle
1 bunch **spring onions**
½ teaspoon **ground turmeric**
400 ml (14 fl oz) can **coconut
milk**
200 g (7 oz) **baby spinach**
300 g (10 oz) **straight-to-wok
rice noodles**

Rub the chicken skin with the seven-spice seasoning.
Heat the oil in a flameproof casserole and fry the
chicken on all sides until lightly browned. Scatter
in the garlic, chilli and ginger and fry for 1 minute.

Add the stock and bring to the boil. Cover and place
in a preheated oven, 180°C (350°F), Gas Mark 4,
for 45 minutes.

Put the lemon grass, fish sauce, sugar and lime juice
in a food processor. Roughly chop the coriander and
spring onions and add to the processor with the
turmeric. Blend until finely chopped. Add the coconut
milk and blend until smooth.

Pour the spicy milk over the chicken and return to
the oven for a further 45 minutes until the chicken is
very tender.

Remove from the oven and stir the spinach and rice
noodles into the sauce around the chicken. Leave to
rest for 10 minutes, then serve.

For homemade chicken stock, put a chicken carcass,
trimmings such as the giblets and the scrapings left
in the pan after a roast in a large saucepan. Add 1
large, unpeeled and halved onion, 1 chopped carrot,
1 celery stick, roughly chopped, several bay leaves and
1 teaspoon of peppercorns. Cover with cold water and
heat until simmering. Cook on the lowest setting,
uncovered, for 1½ hours. Strain through a sieve and
leave to cool.

duck with kumquat honey sauce

Serves **4**
Preparation time **15 minutes**
Cooking time **45 minutes**

4 **duck leg** portions
½ teaspoon **Chinese five-
    spice powder**
300 ml (½ pint) freshly
    squeezed **orange juice**
2 tablespoons **clear honey**
2 **cloves**
1 tablespoon **Cointreau**
    or **brandy**
10 **kumquats**, sliced
1 tablespoon chopped **flat
    leaf parsley**
salt and pepper

Place the duck legs on a rack standing inside a
roasting pan, season well with salt, pepper and the
five-spice powder and roast in a preheated oven,
220°C (425°F), Gas Mark 7, for 35 minutes.

Put the orange juice, honey, cloves, Cointreau or
brandy and kumquats in the roasting pan under the
rack after roasting the duck for 10 minutes. Return
the pan to the oven for the remaining 25 minutes.

Remove the duck from the oven and add to the
roasting pan with the kumquat sauce. Simmer gently
together on the hob for 10 minutes.

Add the chopped parsley to the sauce, thickly slice
the duck and serve piping hot with boiled potatoes
and green beans.

For chicken with pink grapefruit and honey sauce,
use the same quantity of chicken as duck. Replace the
orange juice with the same quantity of grapefruit juice
and use 2 pink grapefruits, segmented, instead of the
kumquats. Increase the honey to 3 tablespoons and
cook as above.

aromatic braised duck

Serves **4**
Preparation time **25 minutes**
Cooking time **2 hours**

4 **duck portions**
2 teaspoons **Chinese
five-spice powder**
2 **lemon grass stalks**,
bruised
5 **garlic cloves**, crushed
4 **red shallots**, chopped
125 g (4 oz) **dried shiitake
mushrooms**, soaked for
30 minutes
5 cm (2 inch) piece of **fresh
root ginger**, peeled and cut
into thick julienne strips
600 ml (1 pint) **chicken stock**
(see page 16)
25 g (1 oz) dried **medlar
berries** or **Chinese red
dates**
15 g (½ oz) **dried black
fungus**, broken into pieces
1 tablespoon **fish sauce**
2 teaspoons **cornflour**
4 **spring onions**, quartered
salt and pepper
handful of **fresh coriander**,
to garnish

Season the duck portions with the five-spice powder.
Place them skin-side down in a very hot frying pan
or casserole to brown the skin. Turn the pieces over.
Add the lemon grass, garlic, shallots, mushrooms and
ginger to the pan, then cover the duck with the stock.
Cover the pan with a lid and simmer very gently for
1½ hours.

Remove the duck from the pan and add the medlar
berries or Chinese red dates, black fungus and fish
sauce. Season with salt and pepper to taste. Mix the
cornflour to a smooth paste with a little water and add
to the pan. Bring the sauce to the boil, stirring
constantly, and cook until thickened. Return the duck
to the pan and simmer gently for 30 minutes.

Add the spring onions to the sauce and garnish the
duck with the coriander.

For stir-fried pak choi to serve as an
accompaniment, heat 1 tablespoon olive oil in a
nonstick sauté pan over a high heat. Add 500 g
(1 lb) pak choi, halved, a handful at a time, stirring
occasionally. Cover the pan and cook for 2–3 minutes
until the bok choi leaves have wilted. Mix together
1 teaspoon tamari sauce, 1 tablespoon Chinese rice
wine and 3 tablespoons vegetable stock (see page
190) in a small bowl. Add a cornflour paste made
from ½ tablespoon cornflour mixed with 1 tablespoon
water and pour over the pak choi, stirring constantly
until the sauce thickens.

garlic butter-stuffed chicken

Serves **4**
Preparation time **25 minutes**
Cooking time **40 minutes**

50 g (2 oz) coarse
   breadcrumbs
3 tablespoons **olive oil**
4 large skinned **chicken
   breast fillets**
25 g (1 oz) **butter**, softened
50 g (2 oz) **cream cheese**
2 **garlic cloves**, crushed
finely grated rind of 1 **lemon**
4 tablespoons chopped
   parsley
150 g (5 oz) **French beans**,
   diagonally sliced into 3.5 cm
   (1½ inch) lengths
400 g (13 oz) can **flageolet
   beans**, drained
200 ml (7 fl oz) **white wine**
salt and pepper

Put the breadcrumbs in a flameproof casserole with 1 tablespoon of the oil and heat gently until the breadcrumbs begin to brown and crisp. Drain to a plate.

Using a small knife, make a horizontal cut in each chicken breast to create a pocket for stuffing.

Beat the butter with the cream cheese, garlic, lemon rind, 1 tablespoon of the parsley and salt and pepper. Pack the stuffing into the chicken breasts and seal the openings with wooden cocktail sticks.

Heat the remaining oil in the casserole and fry the chicken on both sides until lightly browned. Drain. Scatter the French beans and flageolet beans into the casserole and add the wine and a little seasoning. Arrange the chicken on top.

Cover and place in a preheated oven, 190°C (375°F), Gas Mark 5, for 20 minutes. Remove the lid and sprinkle the chicken pieces with the breadcrumbs. Return to the oven, uncovered, for a further 10 minutes until the chicken is cooked through.

Transfer the chicken to plates. Stir the remaining parsley into the beans, then spoon around the chicken.

For roast potatoes with garlic to serve as an accompaniment, heat 50 ml (2 fl oz) olive oil in a roasting pan in a preheated oven, 230°C (450°F), Gas Mark 8. Quarter 750 g (1½ lb) potatoes, then add with 2 tablespoons chopped rosemary to the hot oil, tossing to coat. Roast for 20 minutes. Remove, turn the potatoes, scatter with 4 sliced garlic cloves and return to the oven for a further 10–20 minutes.

chicken, okra & red lentil dhal

Serves **4**
Preparation time **15 minutes**
Cooking time **45 minutes**

2 teaspoons **ground cumin**
1 teaspoon **ground coriander**
½ teaspoon **cayenne pepper**
¼ teaspoon **ground turmeric**
500 g (1 lb) skinned and
  boned **chicken thighs**,
  cut into large pieces
3 tablespoons **oil**
1 **onion**, sliced
2 **garlic cloves**, crushed
25 g (1 oz) **fresh root ginger**,
  finely chopped
750 ml (1¼ pints) **water**
300 g (10 oz) **red lentils**,
  rinsed
200 g (7 oz) **okra**
small handful of **fresh
  coriander**, chopped
salt
lime wedges, to garnish

Mix together the cumin, coriander, cayenne and turmeric and toss with the chicken pieces.

Heat the oil in a large saucepan. Fry the chicken pieces in batches until deep golden, draining each batch to a plate. Add the onion to the pan and fry for 5 minutes until browned. Stir in the garlic and ginger and cook for a further 1 minute.

Return the chicken to the pan and add the measurement water. Bring to the boil, then reduce the heat and simmer very gently, covered, for 20 minutes until the chicken is cooked through. Add the lentils and cook for 5 minutes. Stir in the okra, coriander and a little salt and cook for a further 5 minutes until the lentils are tender but not completely pulpy.

Check the seasoning and serve in shallow bowls with lime wedges, chutney and poppadums.

For chicken, courgette and chilli dhal, use 3 medium courgettes, thinly sliced, instead of the okra. For a hotter flavour, add a thinly sliced medium-strength red chilli with the garlic and ginger.

spiced turkey & pepper wraps

Serves **4**
Preparation time **15 minutes**
Cooking time **40 minutes**

1 teaspoon **mild chilli powder**
½ teaspoon **ground cumin**
1 teaspoon chopped **thyme**
625 g (1¼ lb) lean **turkey breast fillet**, cut into small chunks
4 **mixed peppers**, deseeded and cut into large chunks
2 **red onions**, sliced
4 tablespoons **olive oil**
2 large **courgettes**, cut into chip-sized pieces
1 teaspoon **cornflour**
2 tablespoons **red** or **white wine vinegar**
2 tablespoons **clear honey**
2 tablespoons **sun-dried tomato paste**
few drops **Tabasco sauce**
4 tablespoons **water**
50 g (2 oz) **dried pineapple**, sliced
4 **flour tortillas**, warmed
salt

Mix the chilli powder with the cumin, thyme and a little salt and use to coat the turkey. Scatter in a large roasting pan with the peppers and onions.

Drizzle with the oil and toss the ingredients lightly together. Place the pan in a preheated oven, 220°C (425°F), Gas Mark 7, for 15 minutes. Add the courgettes to the pan, mixing them into the pan juices, and return to the oven for a further 20 minutes until the turkey is cooked through and the vegetables are tender.

Mix together the cornflour and vinegar to make a smooth paste. Add the honey, tomato paste, Tabasco and a little salt and add to the roasting pan with the measurement water. Stir together well. Scatter with the pineapple and return to the oven for a further 2–3 minutes until the glaze has slightly thickened to coat the meat and vegetables. Divide between the warmed tortillas, roll up and serve.

For spiced sweet potato wraps, omit the turkey and use 625 g (1¼ lb) sweet potatoes, thinly sliced and coated in the chilli mixture as above. Replace the onions with 2 bunches spring onions, chopped, and the courgettes with 1 small aubergine, thinly sliced. Add the aubergines with the peppers and spring onions after 15 minutes of the cooking time.

biryani

Serves **4**
Preparation time **25 minutes**
Cooking time **40 minutes**

3 **onions**
2 **garlic cloves**, chopped
25 g (1 oz) **fresh root ginger**,
   roughly chopped
2 teaspoons **ground turmeric**
¼ teaspoon **ground cloves**
½ teaspoon **dried chilli flakes**
¼ teaspoon **ground cinnamon**
2 teaspoons **medium curry
   paste**
1 tablespoon **lemon juice**
2 teaspoons **caster sugar**
300 g (10 oz) lean **chicken,
   turkey breast** or **lamb fillet**,
   cut into small pieces
6 tablespoons **oil**
1 small **cauliflower**, cut into
   small florets
2 **bay leaves**
300 g (10 oz) **basmati rice**
750 ml (1¼ pints) **chicken** or
   vegetable stock (see pages
   16 and 190)
1 tablespoon **black onion
   seeds**
salt and pepper
2 tablespoons toasted flaked
   almonds, to garnish

Roughly chop 1 onion and put in a food processor with the garlic, ginger, turmeric, cloves, chilli flakes, cinnamon, curry paste, lemon juice, sugar and salt and pepper. Blend to a thick paste and turn into a bowl. Add the meat to the bowl and mix together well.

Thinly slice the second onion. Heat 5 tablespoons of the oil in a large frying pan and fry the onion slices until deep golden and crisp. Drain on kitchen paper.

Chop the third onion. Add the cauliflower to the frying pan and fry gently for 5 minutes. Add the chopped onion and fry gently, stirring, for about 5 minutes until the cauliflower is softened and golden. Drain.

Heat the remaining oil in the pan. Tip in the meat and marinade and fry gently for 5 minutes, stirring.

Stir in the bay leaves, rice and stock and bring to the boil. Reduce the heat and simmer very gently, stirring occasionally, for 10–12 minutes until the rice is tender and the stock absorbed, adding a little water to the pan if the mixture is dry before the rice is cooked. Stir in the black onion seeds. Return the cauliflower to the pan and heat through.

Pile on to serving plates and serve scattered with the crisp onion and toasted almonds. Serve with a cucumber raita (see below), if you like.

For cucumber and mint raita, gently mix together the following in a bowl: 175 g (6 oz) natural yogurt, 75 g (3 oz) cucumber, deseeded and coarsely grated, 2 tablespoons chopped mint, 1 pinch ground cumin and lemon juice and salt to taste. Stand for 30 minutes.

venison & chestnut stew

Serves **6**
Preparation time **30 minutes**
Cooking time **2½ hours**

2 tablespoons **plain flour**
875 g (1¾ lb) lean **stewing
    venison**, cut into small
    pieces
10 **juniper berries**
3 tablespoons **oil**
150 g (5 oz) **bacon lardons**
1 **large onion**, chopped
3 **carrots**, sliced
½ teaspoon **ground cloves**
300 ml (½ pint) **red wine**
200 ml (7 fl oz) **game stock**
    or **chicken stock** (see page
    16)
1 tablespoon **red wine
    vinegar**
2 tablespoons **redcurrant jelly**
350 g (12 oz) **cooked
    chestnuts**
1 kg (2 lb) large **potatoes**,
    thinly sliced
2 teaspoons chopped
    rosemary
40 g (1½ oz) **butter**, softened
salt and pepper

Season the flour with salt and pepper and use to coat
the venison. Crush the juniper berries using a pestle
and mortar.

Heat the oil in a large, flameproof casserole and fry
the meat in batches until browned, draining each batch
to a plate. Add the bacon, onion and carrots to the
casserole and fry gently for 5 minutes or until browned.

Stir in the crushed juniper berries, cloves, wine, stock,
vinegar and redcurrant jelly and bring to the boil.
Reduce the heat and stir in the chestnuts and venison.

Cover with a lid and place in a preheated oven, 160°C
(325°F), Gas Mark 3, for 1 hour. Check the seasoning,
then scatter with the potatoes and return to the oven,
covered, for a further 30 minutes.

Blend the rosemary with the butter and a little
seasoning and dot over the potatoes. Return to the
oven, uncovered, for a further 45 minutes or until the
potatoes are lightly browned.

For homemade game stock, brown 500 g (1 lb)
game trimmings (for example pheasant or pigeon
bones) in a roasting pan in a preheated oven, 200°C
(400°F), Gas Mark 6, for 15 minutes. Tip into a
saucepan with 1 unpeeled, roughly chopped onion,
1 chopped carrot, 2 chopped celery sticks, 1 glass
red wine, 1 teaspoon juniper berries and 3 bay leaves.
Cover with water. Bring to a simmer and cook very
gently for 1½ hours. Strain through a sieve and leave
to cool.

noodle soup with chicken

Serves **4–6**
Preparation time **20 minutes**
Cooking time **30 minutes**

300 g (10 oz) skinned and
  boned **chicken breasts**
1 teaspoon **ground turmeric**
2 teaspoons **salt**
2 **lemon grass stalks**
3 tablespoons skinned and
  roasted **peanuts**
3 tablespoons **white long-
  grain rice**
2 tablespoons **vegetable oil**
1 **onion**, chopped
3 **garlic cloves**, crushed
5 cm (2 inch) piece of **fresh
  root ginger**, peeled and
  finely chopped
¼ teaspoon **ground paprika**
1 hot **red bird chilli**, chopped
2 tablespoons **fish sauce**
900 ml (1½ pints) **water**
250 g (8 oz) **straight-to-wok
  wheat noodles** (somen)

To garnish
3 **hard-boiled eggs**, halved
2 tablespoons chopped **fresh
  coriander**
handful **spring onions**,
  shredded

Cut the chicken breasts into 1.5 cm (¾ inch) cubes.
Mix the turmeric with the salt, rub into the cubes of
chicken and leave to stand for 30 minutes.

Bruise the lemon grass with the side of a rolling pin
to release the flavour. Finely crush the roasted peanuts
in a food processor or using a pestle and mortar. Heat
a dry frying pan and toast the rice until golden brown,
then finely crush to a powder in a food processor or
spice grinder.

Heat the oil in a large pan and fry the onion until just
softened. Add the chicken together with the garlic,
ginger, lemon grass, paprika and chilli. Add the fish
sauce and measurement water and bring to the boil.

Reduce the heat to a simmer. Mix together the
crushed peanuts and ground rice and add to the pan.
Simmer for about 10–15 minutes or until the chicken
has cooked through and the broth thickened slightly.

Stir the noodles into the pan and heat for 1 minute.

Ladle the chicken soup into bowls and serve garnished
with the hard-boiled eggs, chopped coriander and
shredded spring onions. Add an extra splash of fish
sauce, to taste.

For prawn and coconut noodle soup, use 400 g
(13 oz) raw peeled prawns instead of the chicken and
add to the pan with the noodles, cooking gently until
they turn pink. Replace the wheat noodles with rice
noodles and omit the hard-boiled eggs.

chicken & pickled walnut pilaf

Serves **4**
Preparation time **20 minutes**
Cooking time **35 minutes**

400 g (13 oz) skinned and
    boned **chicken thighs**, cut
    into small pieces
2 teaspoons **Moroccan spice
    blend**
4 tablespoons **olive oil**
50 g (2 oz) **pine nuts**
1 large **onion**, chopped
3 **garlic cloves**, sliced
½ teaspoon **ground turmeric**
250 g (8 oz) mixed **long-grain**
    and **wild rice**
300 ml (½ pint) **chicken stock**
    (see page 16)
3 pieces of **stem ginger**,
    finely chopped
3 tablespoons chopped
    parsley
2 tablespoons chopped **mint**
50 g (2 oz) **pickled walnuts**,
    sliced
salt and pepper

Toss the chicken pieces in the spice blend and a little salt.

Heat the oil in a large frying pan or sauté pan and fry the pine nuts until they begin to colour. Drain with a slotted spoon.

Add the chicken to the pan and fry gently for 6–8 minutes, stirring until lightly browned.

Stir in the onion and fry gently for 5 minutes. Add the garlic and turmeric and fry for a further 1 minute. Add the rice and stock and bring to the boil. Reduce the heat to its lowest setting and simmer very gently for about 15 minutes until the rice is tender and the stock absorbed. Add a little water if the liquid has been absorbed before the rice is cooked through.

Stir in the ginger, parsley, mint, walnuts and pine nuts. Season to taste and heat through gently for 2 minutes before serving.

For homemade Moroccan spice blend, mix together ½ teaspoon each of crushed fennel, cumin, coriander and mustard seeds with ¼ teaspoon each of ground cloves and cinnamon.

chicken & mushrooms with polenta

Serves **4**
Preparation time **20 minutes**
Cooking time **55 minutes**

25 g (1 oz) **butter**
1 **onion**, chopped
500 g (1 lb) lean **chicken**,
  diced
250 g (8 oz) **mushrooms**,
  sliced
2 teaspoons **plain flour**
150 ml (¼ pint) **chicken stock**
  (see page 16)
1 tablespoon **grainy mustard**
4 tablespoons chopped
  parsley
100 ml (3½ fl oz) **single
  cream**
200 g (7 oz) **fresh soya
  beans** or 400 g (13 oz) can
  flageolet beans, drained
500 g (1 lb) pack **ready-
  cooked polenta**
50 g (2 oz) **Gruyère cheese**,
  grated
salt and pepper

Melt the butter in a shallow, flameproof casserole. Add the onion and chicken and fry gently for 6–8 minutes, stirring frequently, until lightly browned.

Add the mushrooms and fry for a further 5 minutes. Sprinkle in the flour, then add the stock, mustard, parsley and a little seasoning. Bring to the boil, then reduce the heat and stir in the cream and beans.

Slice the polenta very thinly and arrange, overlapping the slices, on top of the chicken. Sprinkle with the cheese and a little black pepper.

Place in a preheated oven, 190°C (375°F), Gas Mark 5, for 30–40 minutes until the cheese is melted and beginning to brown. Serve with a leafy salad.

For chicken and mushrooms with cheese toasts, replace the polenta with 8 thin slices of French bread. Arrange over the chicken, then sprinkle with the same quantity of Cheddar cheese instead of the Gruyère. Cook as above, until the cheese has melted and the bread is turning golden.

stifado

Serves **3–4**
Preparation time **20 minutes**
Cooking time **2½ hours**

½ teaspoon **ground black pepper**
½ teaspoon **ground allspice**
2 teaspoons finely chopped **rosemary**
1 **rabbit** (about 750–875 g/ 1½–1¾ lb), jointed
3 tablespoons **olive oil**
3 large **onions**, sliced
2 teaspoons **caster sugar**
3 **garlic cloves**, crushed
75 ml (3 fl oz) **red wine vinegar**
300 ml (½ pint) **red wine**
50 g (2 oz) **tomato purée**
salt
flat leaf parsley, to sprinkle

Mix together the pepper, allspice and rosemary and rub over the rabbit.

Heat the oil in a large, flameproof casserole and fry the meat in batches on all sides until thoroughly browned. Drain the meat to a plate.

Add the onions to the pan with the sugar and fry, stirring frequently, for about 15 minutes until caramelized. Stir in the garlic and then cook for a further 1 minute.

Add the vinegar and wine to the pan. Bring to the boil and continue to boil until the mixture has reduced by about a third. Stir in the tomato purée and a little salt and return the meat to the pan.

Cover with a lid and place in a preheated oven, 150°C (300°F), Gas Mark 2, for about 2 hours until the meat is very tender and the juices thick and glossy. Check the seasoning and sprinkle with the parsley.

For Greek salad to serve as an accompaniment, combine 6 roughly chopped tomatoes, 1 thickly sliced cucumber, ½ small, thinly sliced red onion and 125 g (4 oz) kalamata olives together in a large bowl. Drizzle with olive oil and lemon juice to taste. Crumble 200 g (8 oz) feta cheese into pieces and scatter over the salad. Season with plenty of black pepper.

turkey chilli poblano

Serves **6**
Preparation time **25 minutes**
Cooking time **1 hour**

125 g (4 oz) **flaked almonds**
50 g (2 oz) **peanuts**
½ tablespoon **coriander
  seeds**
1 teaspoon **ground cloves**
3 tablespoons **sesame seeds**
½ **cinnamon stick**
1 teaspoon **fennel seeds** or
  aniseed
4 large **dried chillies**
1 **green jalapeño chilli**,
  chopped
400 g (13 oz) can **chopped
  tomatoes**
75 g (3 oz) **raisins**
6 tablespoons **vegetable oil**
2 **onions**, finely chopped
3 **garlic cloves**, crushed
625 g (1¼ lb) **turkey fillets**,
  finely sliced or cubed
300 ml (½ pint) **vegetable
  stock** (see page 190)
50 g (2 oz) **bitter plain
  chocolate**, roughly chopped

To garnish
red and green chillies, finely
  chopped

Spread the almonds, peanuts, coriander seeds, cloves, sesame seeds, cinnamon, fennel or aniseed and dried chillies over a baking sheet and roast in a preheated oven, 200°C (400°F), Gas Mark 6, for 10 minutes, stirring once or twice.

Remove from the oven and put the nuts and spices in a food processor or blender and process until well combined. Add the chopped green chilli and process once more until well mixed.

Spoon the spice mixture into a bowl and mix in the tomatoes and raisins.

Heat the oil in a large saucepan and fry the onions and garlic with the turkey on all sides until browned. Remove the turkey and set aside.

Add the spice mixture to the oil remaining in the saucepan and cook, stirring frequently, for 5–6 minutes or until the spice paste has heated through and is bubbling. Add the stock and chocolate and simmer gently until the chocolate has melted.

Reduce the heat, return the turkey to the pan and mix well. Cover the pan and simmer gently for 30 minutes, adding extra water if the sauce begins to dry out. Garnish with the chopped red and green chillies.

For Mexican-style rice to serve as an accompaniment, gently heat 2 tablespoons vegetable oil in a saucepan and cook 325 g (11 oz) basmati rice for 5 minutes, stirring. Add 200 g (7 oz) chopped tomatoes, 1 crushed garlic clove, 50 g (2 oz) diced carrot and 1 chopped green chilli. Bring to boil, then simmer for 10 minutes.

spring braised duck

Serves **4**
Preparation time **20 minutes**
Cooking time **1¾ hours**

4 **duck legs**
2 teaspoons **plain flour**
25 g (1 oz) **butter**
1 tablespoon **olive oil**
2 **onions**, sliced
2 **streaky bacon** rashers,
 finely chopped
2 **garlic cloves**, crushed
1 glass **white wine**, about
 150 ml (¼ pint)
300 ml (½ pint) **chicken stock**
 (see page 16)
3 **bay leaves**
500 g (1 lb) small **new
 potatoes,** e.g. Jersey Royals
200 g (7 oz) **fresh peas**
150 g (5 oz) **asparagus tips**
2 tablespoons chopped **mint**
salt and pepper

Halve the duck legs through the joints. Mix the flour with a little seasoning and use to coat the duck pieces.

Melt the butter with the oil in a sturdy roasting pan or flameproof casserole and gently fry the duck pieces for about 10 minutes until browned. Drain to a plate and pour off all but 1 tablespoon of the fat left in the pan.

Add the onions and bacon to the pan and fry gently for 5 minutes. Add the garlic and fry for a further 1 minute. Add the wine, stock and bay leaves and bring to the boil, stirring. Return the duck pieces and cover with a lid or foil. Place in a preheated oven, 160°C (325°F), Gas Mark 3, for 45 minutes.

Add the potatoes to the pan, stirring them into the juices. Sprinkle with salt and return to the oven for 30 minutes.

Add the peas, asparagus and mint to the pan and return to the oven for a further 15 minutes or until all the vegetables are tender. Check the seasoning and serve.

For spring braised chicken, replace the duck with 4 chicken thighs and omit the bacon. Add the following spring vegetables when adding the peas, asparagus and mint: 200 g (7 oz) baby turnips, 100 g (3½ oz) baby carrots, 2 small, sliced courgettes. Cook as above.

sweet-glazed chicken

Serves **4**
Preparation time **10 minutes**
Cooking time **45 minutes**

2 tablespoons **olive oil**
4 skinned and boned **chicken breasts**, about 150 g (5 oz) each
8 **fresh apricots**, halved and stoned
2 **pears**, peeled, quartered and cored
500 g (1 lb) **new potatoes**
1 **onion**, cut into wedges
grated **rind** and juice of 2 **oranges**
a few **thyme sprigs**, chopped
1 tablespoon **wholegrain mustard**
1 tablespoon **clear honey**
4 tablespoons **crème fraîche**
pepper

Heat the oil in a flameproof casserole, season the chicken with salt and pepper and add to the pan. Fry for 2–3 minutes on each side until golden, then add the apricots, pears, potatoes and onion.

Mix together the orange rind and juice, thyme, mustard and honey and pour over the chicken. Cover the dish with foil and bake in a preheated oven, 180°C (350°F), Gas Mark 4, for 40 minutes, removing the foil halfway through the cooking time.

When the chicken is cooked, stir the crème fraîche into the sauce before serving.

For wilted spinach with pine nuts and raisins to serve as an accompaniment, place 65 g (2½ oz) raisins in a small heatproof bowl, cover with boiling water and leave for 5 minutes. Meanwhile, heat 3 tablespoons olive oil in a frying pan and fry 50 g (2 oz) pine nuts until pale golden. Stir in 2 crushed garlic cloves. Drain the raisins and add to the pan with 625 g (1¼ lb) baby spinach. Cook for 1 minute, turning until the spinach has wilted. Add grated lemon rind and salt and pepper to taste.

chicken, lemon & olive stew

Serves **4**
Preparation time **20 minutes**
Cooking time **1 hour**

1.5 kg (3 lb) **chicken**
about 4 tablespoons **olive oil**
12 **baby onions**, peeled but
  left whole
2 **garlic cloves**, crushed
1 teaspoon each **ground
  cumin, ginger** and **turmeric**
½ teaspoon **ground cinnamon**
450 ml (¾ pint) **chicken stock**
  (see page 16)
125 g (4 oz) **kalamata olives**
1 **preserved lemon**, pulp and
  skin discarded, chopped
2 tablespoons chopped **fresh
  coriander**
salt and pepper

Joint the chicken into 8 pieces (or ask your butcher to do this for you). Heat the oil in a flameproof casserole and brown the chicken on all sides. Remove the pieces with a slotted spoon and set aside.

Add the onions, garlic and spices and sauté over a low heat for 10 minutes until just golden. Return the chicken to the pan, stir in the stock and bring to the boil. Cover and simmer gently for 30 minutes.

Add the olives, preserved lemon and coriander and cook for a further 15–20 minutes until the chicken is really tender. Taste and adjust the seasoning, if necessary.

For green couscous to serve as an accompaniment, shake together 150 ml (¼ pint) olive oil and 50 ml (2 fl oz) lemon juice until well combined. Season with salt and pepper. Tip 250 g (8 oz) cooked couscous (see page 13), into a warmed serving dish and stir in 1 bunch chopped spring onions, 50 g (2 oz) chopped rocket and ½ cucumber, halved, deseeded and chopped. Stir in the lemon juice dressing and serve.

noodles & seven-spice chicken

Serves **4**
Preparation time **15 minutes**
Cooking time **12 minutes**

3 pieces of **stem ginger** from
  a jar, plus 3 tablespoons of
  the syrup
2 tablespoons **rice wine**
  vinegar
3 tablespoons **light soy**
  sauce
4 skinned and boned **chicken**
  breasts, about 150 g (5 oz)
  – 175 g (6 oz) each
1 tablespoon **Thai seven-**
  spice seasoning
3 tablespoons **stir-fry** or **wok**
  oil (see page 11)
3 **shallots**, thinly sliced
125 g (4 oz) **baby corn**,
  halved
300 g (10 oz) **straight-to-wok**
  medium or **thread noodles**
300 g (10 oz) **baby spinach**
200 g (7 oz) **bean sprouts**

Finely shred the pieces of stem ginger. Mix the ginger syrup with the vinegar and soy sauce and reserve.

Halve each chicken breast horizontally and then cut widthways into thin strips. Toss with the seven-spice seasoning.

Heat the oil in a large frying pan or wok and stir-fry the chicken pieces over a gentle heat for 5 minutes until beginning to brown.

Add the shallots and fry for 2 minutes. Stir in the baby corn and fry for 1 minute. Add the noodles and spinach and scatter with the shredded stem ginger. Stir-fry, mixing the ingredients together, until the spinach starts to wilt.

Add the bean sprouts and soy sauce mixture and cook, stirring, for a further 1 minute or until heated through. Serve immediately.

For noodles with seven-spice prawn, replace the chicken with 400 g (13 oz) peeled and deveined raw prawns, toss with the seven-spice seasoning and cook as above. Replace the spinach with 200 g (7 oz) roughly chopped pak choi.

chicken with cornmeal dumplings

Serves **4**

Preparation time **25 minutes**

Cooking time 1½ **hours**

3 tablespoons **olive oil**

8 skinned and boned **chicken thighs**, cut into small pieces

4 teaspoons **Cajun spice blend**

1 large **onion**, sliced

100 g (3½ oz) **smoked streaky bacon**, chopped

2 each **red** and **yellow peppers**, deseeded and roughly chopped

200 ml (7 fl oz) **chicken stock** (see page 16)

125 g (4 oz) **self-raising flour**

125 g (4 oz) **cornmeal**

½ teaspoon **dried chilli flakes**

3 tablespoons chopped **fresh coriander**

75 g (3 oz) **Cheddar cheese**, grated

50 g (2 oz) **butter**, melted

1 egg

100 ml (3½ fl oz) **milk**

4 small **tomatoes**, skinned and quartered

100 ml (3½ fl oz) **double cream**

salt and pepper

Heat the oil in a large, shallow flameproof casserole and fry the chicken pieces for about 5 minutes until lightly browned. Stir in the spice blend and cook for a further 1 minute. Drain to a plate.

Add the onion, bacon and peppers and fry for 10 minutes, stirring frequently, until beginning to colour.

Return the chicken to the casserole and stir in the stock and a little seasoning. Bring to the boil, then cover with a lid and bake in a preheated oven, 180°C (350°F), Gas Mark 4, for 45 minutes until the chicken is tender.

While the chicken is cooking, prepare the dumplings: mix together the flour, cornmeal, chilli flakes, coriander and cheese in a bowl. Beat the butter with the egg and milk and add to the bowl. Mix together to make a thick paste, that is fairly sticky but holds its shape.

Stir the tomatoes and cream into the chicken mixture and season to taste. Place spoonfuls of the dumpling mixture over the top. Return to the oven, uncovered, for a further 30 minutes or until the dumplings have slightly risen and form a firm crust.

For traditional dumplings, mix together 175 g (6 oz) self-raising flour, 50 g (2 oz) vegetable suet and 4 tablespoons chopped parsley in a bowl with a little salt and pepper. Add enough water to mix to a soft, slightly sticky dough. Spoon over the casserole and cook, covered, for 20–25 minutes until the dumplings are light and fluffy.

chicken & tarragon risotto

Serves **6**
Preparation time **15 minutes**
Cooking time **30 minutes**

500 g (1lb) skinned **chicken
  breast fillets**, cut into small
  chunks
25 g (1 oz) **butter**
1 **onion**, finely chopped
2 **garlic cloves**, crushed
300 g (10 oz) **risotto rice**
1 glass **white wine**, about
  150 ml (¼ pint)
400 ml (14 fl oz) **chicken
  stock** or **vegetable stock**
  (see pages 16 and 190)
1 teaspoon **saffron threads**
250 g (8 oz) **mascarpone
  cheese**
3 tablespoons roughly
  chopped **tarragon**
3 tablespoons chopped
  parsley
100 g (3½ oz) **mangetout** or
  sugarsnap peas, halved
salt and pepper

Season the chicken with salt and pepper. Melt the butter in a flameproof casserole, then add the chicken and gently fry for 5 minutes until lightly browned. Add the onion and cook for a further 5 minutes. Add the garlic and rice and cook for a further 1 minute, stirring.

Pour in the wine and let the mixture bubble until the wine has almost evaporated. Stir in the stock and saffron and bring to the boil.

Cover with a lid and bake in a preheated oven, 180°C (350°F), Gas Mark 4, for 10 minutes until the stock is absorbed and the rice is almost tender.

Stir in the mascarpone, tarragon, parsley and mangetout or peas. Mix well until the cheese has melted, then cover and return to the oven for a further 5 minutes. Stir in a little boiling water if the mixture has dried out. Check the seasoning and serve with a leafy salad.

For creamy swordfish and tarragon risotto, replace the chicken with 4 swordfish fillets, cut into chunks, and fry off as above in the first step. Replace the mascarpone with 150 ml (¼ pint) single cream.

coq au vin

Serves **6–8**
Preparation time: **20 minutes**
Cooking time: 1½ **hours**

3 tablespoons **oil**
3–4 slices of **bread**, crusts
  removed, diced
50 g (2 oz) **butter**
2.5 kg (5 lb) **chicken**, cut into
  12 serving pieces
24 **small pickling onions**,
  peeled
125 g (4 oz) **smoked bacon**,
  diced
1 tablespoon **plain flour**
1 bottle **red wine**
1 **bouquet garni**
2 **garlic cloves**, peeled
freshly grated **nutmeg**
24 **button mushrooms**, sliced
1 tablespoon **brandy**
salt and pepper

To garnish
chopped **parsley**
pared strips of **orange rind**

Heat 1 tablespoon of the oil in a large, flameproof casserole and fry the bread until golden. Drain. Add the remaining oil, the butter and chicken pieces. Fry gently over a low heat until golden on all sides, turning occasionally. Remove with a slotted spoon and keep warm. Pour off a little of the fat from the casserole, then add the onions and bacon. Sauté until lightly coloured, then sprinkle in the flour and stir well.

Pour in the wine and bring to the boil, stirring. Add the bouquet garni, garlic cloves, nutmeg and salt and pepper to taste. Return the chicken to the casserole. Reduce the heat, cover and simmer for 15 minutes.

Add the mushrooms and continue cooking gently for a further 45 minutes or until the chicken is cooked and tender. Remove the chicken with a slotted spoon and arrange the pieces on a warmed serving plate. Keep hot. Pour the brandy into the sauce and boil, uncovered, for 5 minutes until the sauce is thick and reduced. Remove the bouquet garni and garlic cloves.

Pour the sauce over the chicken and serve with the bread croûtes. Garnish with the chopped parsley and orange rind.

For creamy mashed potatoes to serve as an accompaniment, cook 8 large potatoes, cut into chunks, in a saucepan of salted boiling water for 20 minutes. Mash, then beat until very smooth. Add 50 g (2 oz) butter, then gradually beat in 75 ml (3 fl oz) hot milk until fluffy. Season and add a pinch of nutmeg.

guinea fowl & bean soup

Serves **4–6**
Preparation time **20 minutes,**
  plus overnight soaking
Cooking time **1½ hours**

250 g (8 oz) **dried**
  black-eyed beans
1 kg (2 lb) oven-ready **guinea**
  fowl
1 **onion**, sliced
2 **garlic cloves**, crushed
1.5 litres (2½ pints) **chicken**
  stock (see page 16)
½ teaspoon **ground cloves**
50 g (2 oz) can **anchovies,**
  drained and finely chopped
100 g (3½ oz) **watercress**
150 g (5 oz) **wild**
  mushrooms
3 tablespoons **tomato purée**
salt and pepper

Put the beans in a bowl, cover with plenty of cold water and leave to soak overnight.

Drain the beans and put in a large saucepan. Cover with water and bring to the boil. Boil for 10 minutes, then drain the beans through a colander.

Put the guinea fowl in the pan and add the drained beans, onion, garlic, stock and cloves. Bring just to the boil, then reduce the heat to its lowest setting and cover with a lid. Cook very gently for 1¼ hours until the guinea fowl is very tender.

Drain the guinea fowl to a plate and leave until cool enough to handle. Flake all the meat from the bones, discarding the skin. Chop up any large pieces of meat and return all the meat to the pan.

Scoop a little of the stock into a small bowl with the anchovies and mix together so that the anchovies are blended with the stock. Discard the tough stalks from the watercress.

Add the anchovy mixture, mushrooms and tomato purée to the pan and season with salt and plenty of black pepper. Reheat gently for a few minutes and stir in the watercress just before serving.

For chicken and haricot bean soup, use the same quantity of haricot beans rather than the black-eyed. Take 4 chicken legs, cook and flake the meat from the bones as above. Finally, replace the watercress with the same quantity of rocket, chopped.

game & chestnut casserole

Serves **6**
Preparation time **40 minutes**
Cooking time **1 hour 40 minutes**

500 g (1 lb) **pork sausagemeat**
3 **onions**, finely chopped
2 tablespoons chopped **thyme**
400 g (13 oz) **mixed game**,
350 g (12 oz) **mixed poultry**,
2 tablespoons **plain flour**
100 g (3½ oz) **butter**
2 **celery sticks**, chopped
2 **garlic cloves**, crushed
750 ml (1¼ pints) **chicken** or **game stock** (see pages 16 and 30)
10 **juniper berries**, crushed
200 g (7 oz) **self-raising flour**
1 teaspoon **baking powder**
Approx 150 ml (½ pint) **milk**, plus a little extra to glaze
200 g (7 oz) whole **cooked chestnuts**
3 tablespoons **Worcestershire sauce**
salt and pepper

Mix the sausagemeat with one-third of the onions, half the thyme and plenty of seasoning. Shape into balls about 1.5 cm (¾ inch) in diameter.

Cut all the meat into small pieces. Season the plain flour and use to coat the meat. Melt 25 g (1 oz) of the butter in a large, flameproof casserole and brown the meat in batches, draining each batch to a plate.

Melt another 25 g (1 oz) of the butter and fry the remaining onions and the celery for 5 minutes. Add the garlic and fry for 1 minute. Stir in any remaining coating flour, then blend in the stock. Return the meat to the pan with the juniper berries. Cover and place in a preheated oven, 160°C (325°F), Gas Mark 3, for 1 hour until the meat is tender.

Meanwhile, put the self-raising flour and baking powder in a food processor with a little salt, the remaining thyme and the remaining butter, cut into pieces. Blend to breadcrumb consistency. Add most of the milk to make a dough, adding the rest if it is very dry. Turn out on to a floured surface and roll out to 1.5 cm (¾ inch) thick. Cut out rounds using a 4 cm (1¾ inch) cutter.

Stir the chestnuts and the Worcestershire sauce into the casserole and check the seasoning. Arrange the scones around the edge and glaze with milk. Raise the oven temperature to 220°C (425°F), Gas Mark 7, and cook for 20 minutes or until the scones are cooked through.

quail with chorizo & peppers

Serves **2**
Preparation time **15 minutes**
Cooking time **45 minutes**

25 g (1 oz) **butter**
1 tablespoon **olive oil**
1 **onion**, finely chopped
75 g (3 oz) **chorizo**, finely
   diced
2 plump **quails**
1 **green pepper**, deseeded
   and finely chopped
1 **red pepper**, deseeded and
   finely chopped
2 tablespoons **sun-dried**
   tomato paste
1 tablespoon **clear honey**
100 ml (3½ fl oz) **medium**
   sherry
salt and pepper

Melt the butter with the oil in a flameproof casserole and gently fry the onion and chorizo for 5 minutes until beginning to brown.

Add the quails to the pan and fry in the oil mixture, turning frequently, until seared on all sides and beginning to colour. Drain the quails to a plate.

Add the peppers and fry for 5 minutes, turning them in the oil mixture. Stir in the tomato paste. Return the quails to the pan and brush with the honey. Pour the sherry over and season with salt and pepper.

Cover with a lid and transfer to a preheated oven, 180°C (350°F), Gas Mark 4, for 30 minutes until the quails are cooked through. Test by piercing a thick area of flesh with the tip of a sharp knife; it should feel very tender. Check the seasoning and transfer the pepper sauce to serving plates. Place the quails on top and spoon any cooking juices over them.

For aromatic herb couscous to serve as an accompaniment, put 125 g (4 oz) couscous in a heatproof bowl. Add 150 ml (½ pint) chicken or vegetable stock (see pages 16 and 190), cover and leave to stand in a warm place for 10 minutes. Stir in the finely grated rind of 1 lemon, ¼ teaspoon smoked paprika, 2 tablespoons chopped parsely and 1 tablespoon chopped mint. Season to taste and fluff up with a fork.

chicken & spinach masala

Serves **4**
Preparation time **15 minutes**
Cooking time **13–16 minutes**

2 tablespoons **oil**
1 **onion**, thinly sliced
2 **garlic cloves**, crushed
1 **green chilli**, deseeded and
  thinly sliced
1 teaspoon finely grated **fresh
  root ginger**
1 teaspoon **ground coriander**
1 teaspoon **ground cumin**
200 g (7 oz) can **tomatoes**
750 g (1½ lb) **chicken thighs**,
  skinned, boned and cut into
  bite-sized chunks
200 ml (7 fl oz) **crème fraîche**
300 g (10 oz) **spinach**,
  roughly chopped
2 tablespoons chopped **fresh
  coriander**
salt and pepper

Heat the oil in a large, heavy-based saucepan. Add the onion, garlic, chilli and ginger. Stir-fry for 2–3 minutes and then add the ground coriander and cumin. Stir and cook for a further 1 minute.

Pour in the tomatoes and cook gently for 3 minutes. Increase the heat and add the chicken. Cook, stirring, until the outside of the chicken is sealed. Stir in the crème fraîche and spinach.

Cover the pan and cook the chicken mixture gently for 6–8 minutes, stirring occasionally. Stir in the chopped coriander with seasoning to taste.

For spiced lemon rice to serve as an accompaniment, place 200 g (7 oz) basmati rice in a sieve and wash thoroughly under cold running water. Drain and set aside. Heat 1 tablespoon olive oil in a nonstick saucepan and when hot add 12–14 curry leaves, 1 dried red chilli, ½ cinnamon stick, 2–3 cloves, 4–6 cardamom pods, 2 teaspoons cumin seeds and ¼ teaspoon ground turmeric. Stir-fry for 20-30 seconds, then add the rice. Stir-fry for 2 minutes, then add the juice of 1 large lemon and 450 ml (¾ pint) boiling water. Bring to the boil, cover the pan and reduce the heat to low. Cook for 10–12 minutes, remove from heat and allow to stand for 10 minutes, then fluff up with a fork before serving.

italian chicken with tomato sauce

Serves **4**
Preparation time **20 minutes**
Cooking time **1¼ hours**

4 **chicken legs**, halved
   through the joints
4 tablespoons **olive oil**
1 large **onion**, finely chopped
1 **celery stick**, finely chopped
75 g (3 oz) **pancetta**, diced
2 **garlic cloves**, crushed
3 **bay leaves**
4 tablespoons **dry vermouth**
   or **white wine**
2 x 400 g (13 oz) cans
   chopped tomatoes
1 teaspoon **caster sugar**
3 tablespoons **sun-dried**
   tomato paste
25 g (1 oz) **basil leaves**, torn
   into pieces
8 **black olives**
salt and pepper

Season the chicken pieces with salt and pepper. Heat the oil in a large saucepan or sauté pan and fry the chicken pieces on all sides to brown. Drain to a plate.

Add the onion, celery and pancetta to the pan and fry gently for 10 minutes. Add the garlic and bay leaves and fry for a further 1 minute.

Add the vermouth or wine, tomatoes, sugar, tomato paste and seasoning and bring to the boil. Return the chicken pieces to the pan and reduce the heat to its lowest setting. Cook very gently, uncovered, for about 1 hour or until the chicken is very tender.

Stir in the basil and olives and check the seasoning before serving.

For fennel, orange and olive salad to serve as an accompaniment, toss 1 large fennel bulb, thinly sliced, with 8–10 black olives, 1 tablespoon olive oil and 2 tablespoons lemon juice in a large bowl. Season with salt and pepper. Cut away the skin and pith of 2 oranges and slice thinly into rounds. Add the orange slices to the salad and toss gently to combine.

fish

crayfish risotto

Serves **4**
Preparation time **10 minutes**
Cooking time **30 minutes**

50 g (2 oz) **butter**
2 **shallots**, finely chopped
1 **mild red chilli**, thinly sliced
1 teaspoon **mild paprika**
1 **garlic clove**, crushed
300 g (10 oz) **risotto rice**
1 glass **dry white wine**, about
  150 ml (¼ pint)
a few **lemon thyme sprigs**
about 1.2 litres (2 pints) hot
  fish stock or **chicken stock**
  (see pages 88 and 16)
3 tablespoons roughly
  chopped **tarragon**
300 g (10 oz) **crayfish tails** in
  brine, drained
salt
freshly grated **Parmesan**
  cheese, to garnish

Melt half the butter in a large saucepan or deep-sided sauté pan and gently fry the shallots until softened. Add the chilli, paprika and garlic and fry gently for 30 seconds, without browning the garlic.

Sprinkle in the rice and fry gently for 1 minute, stirring. Add the wine and let it bubble until almost evaporated.

Add the thyme and a ladleful of the stock and cook, stirring, until the rice has almost absorbed the stock. Continue cooking, adding the stock a ladleful at a time, and letting the rice absorb most of the stock before adding more. Once the rice is tender but retaining a little bite, the risotto is ready – this will take about 25 minutes. You may not need all the stock.

Stir in the tarragon, crayfish and remaining butter and heat through gently for 1 minute. Add a little extra salt if necessary and serve immediately, garnished with Parmesan and with a watercress salad, if you like.

For prawn risotto, cook 350 g (11½ oz) raw peeled prawns in the butter, as in the first step. Cook until pink, drain, then return to the pan in the fourth step. Omit the chilli and replace the shallots with 1 bunch chopped spring onions.

monkfish with coconut rice

Serves **4**
Preparation time **20 minutes**
Cooking time **25 minutes**

625 g (1¼ lb) **monkfish fillets**
4 long, slender **lemon grass stalks**
1 bunch **spring onions**
3 tablespoons **stir-fry** or **wok oil** (see page 11)
½ teaspoon **crushed dried chillies**
2 **garlic cloves**, sliced
300 g (10 oz) **Thai fragrant rice**
400 g (13 oz) can **coconut milk**
50 g (2 oz) **creamed coconut**, chopped
200 ml (7 fl oz) **hot water**
2 tablespoons **rice wine vinegar**
150 g (5 oz) **baby spinach**
salt and pepper

Cut the monkfish into 3 cm (1¼ inch) cubes. Using a large knife, slice each lemon grass stalk in half lengthways. (If the stalks are very thick, pull off the outer layers, finely chop them and add to the oil with the chilli flakes.) Cut the thin ends of each stalk to a point and thread the monkfish on to the skewers. If it is difficult to thread the fish, pierce each piece with a small knife first to make threading easier.

Finely chop the spring onions, keeping the white and green parts separate.

Heat the oil in a large frying pan with the chilli flakes, garlic and white parts of the spring onions. Add the monkfish skewers and fry gently for about 5 minutes, turning once, until cooked through. Drain to a plate.

Add the rice, coconut milk and creamed coconut to the frying pan and bring to the boil. Reduce the heat, cover with a lid or foil and cook gently for 6–8 minutes, stirring frequently, until the rice is almost tender and the milk absorbed. Add the measurement water and cook, covered, for a further 10 minutes until the rice is completely tender, adding a little more water if the mixture boils dry before the rice is tender.

Stir in the vinegar, remaining spring onions and then the spinach, turning it in the rice until wilted. Arrange the skewers over the rice. Cover and cook gently for 3 minutes, then serve immediately.

pot-roasted tuna with lentils

Serves **4**

Preparation time **15 minutes**

Cooking time **50 minutes –
    1 hour 5 minutes**

½ teaspoon **celery salt**

750 g (1½ lb) **tuna**, in one
    slender piece

1 **fennel bulb**

3 tablespoons **olive oil**

250 g (8 oz) **black lentils**,
    rinsed

1 glass **white wine**, about
    150 ml (¼ pint)

250 ml (8 fl oz) **fish stock** or
    vegetable stock (see pages
    88 and 190)

4 tablespoons chopped
    fennel leaves or **dill**

2 tablespoons **capers**, rinsed
    and drained

400 g (13 oz) can **chopped
    tomatoes**

salt and pepper

Mix the celery salt with a little pepper and rub all over
the tuna. Cut the fennel bulb in half, then into thin slices.

Heat the oil in a flameproof casserole and fry the tuna
on all sides until browned. Drain. Add the sliced fennel
to the pan and fry gently until softened.

Add the lentils and wine and bring to the boil. Boil until
the wine has reduced by about half. Stir in the stock,
fennel leaves or dill, capers and tomatoes and return
to the boil. Cover with a lid and transfer to a preheated
oven, 180°C (350°F), Gas Mark 4, for 15 minutes.

Return the tuna to the casserole and cook gently
for a further 20 minutes until the lentils are completely
tender. The tuna should still be slightly pink in the
centre. If you prefer it well done, return to the oven
for a further 15–20 minutes. Check the seasoning
and serve.

For pot-roasted lamb with lentils, replace the tuna
with a 625 g (1¼ lb) piece of rolled loin of lamb. Fry
off the lamb as above in the second step. Omit the
fennel bulb and use the same quantity of chicken
stock instead of the fish or vegetable stock. Replace
the fennel or dill with the same quantity of rosemary or
oregano. Continue as above, cooking for 30 minutes
instead of 20. If you prefer your lamb well done, return
to the oven for a further 20 minutes.

seafood hotpot

Serves **4**
Preparation time **25 minutes**
Cooking time **15 minutes**

1 teaspoon **sesame oil**
1 tablespoon **vegetable oil**
3 **shallots**, chopped
3 **garlic cloves**, crushed
1 **onion**, sliced
150 ml (¼ pint) **coconut milk**
150 ml (¼ pint) **water**
3 tablespoons **rice wine
  vinegar**
1 **lemon grass stalk**, chopped
4 **kaffir lime leaves**
1 **red chilli**, chopped
300 ml (½ pint) **fish stock**
  (see page 88) or **water**
1 tablespoon **caster sugar**
2 **tomatoes**, quartered
4 tablespoons **fish sauce**
1 teaspoon **tomato purée**
375 g (12 oz) **straight-to-wok
  rice noodles**
375 g (12 oz) **tiger prawns**,
  heads removed and peeled
125 g (4 oz) **squid**, cleaned
  and cut into rings
175 g (6 oz) **clams**, scrubbed
400 g (13 oz) can **straw
  mushrooms**, drained
20 **basil leaves**

Heat the sesame and vegetable oils together in a large pan, add the shallots and garlic and fry gently for 2 minutes or until softened but not browned.

Add the onion, coconut milk, measurement water, vinegar, lemon grass, lime leaves, chilli, stock or water and sugar to the pan, bring to the boil and boil for 2 minutes. Reduce the heat and add the tomatoes, fish sauce and tomato purée and cook for 5 minutes. Stir in the rice noodles.

Add the prawns, squid rings, clams and mushrooms to the hotpot and simmer gently for 5–6 minutes or until the seafood is cooked. Stir in the basil leaves. Serve the hotpot immediately.

For nuoc mam dipping sauce to serve as an accompaniment, mix the following ingredients together: 6 tablespoons fish sauce, 2 teaspoons caster sugar, 1 tablespoon rice wine vinegar, 3 finely chopped hot red chillies, 2 finely chopped hot green chillies. Leave to stand for 1 hour.

rich fish stew

Serves **4**

Preparation time **25 minutes**

Cooking time **40 minutes**

4 tablespoons **olive oil**

1 **onion**, chopped

1 small **leek**, chopped

4 **garlic cloves**, crushed

1 teaspoon **saffron threads**

400 g (13 oz) can **chopped tomatoes**

4 tablespoons **sun-dried tomato paste**

1 litre (1¾ pints) **fish stock** (see page 88)

3 **bay leaves**

several **thyme sprigs**

750 g (1½ lb) **mixed fish**, e.g. **haddock**, **bream**, **halibut**, **bass**, skinned, boned and cut into chunky pieces

250 g (8 oz) **raw peeled prawns**

salt and pepper

8 tablespoons **aïoli** and baguette slices, to garnish

Heat the oil in a large saucepan and gently fry the onion and leek for 5 minutes. Add the garlic and fry for a further 1 minute.

Stir in the saffron, tomatoes, tomato paste, stock, bay leaves and thyme. Bring to the boil, then reduce the heat and simmer gently for 25 minutes.

Gently stir in the mixed fish and cook very gently for 5 minutes. Stir in the prawns and cook for a further 2–3 minutes until the prawns have turned pink and the fish flakes easily when pierced with a knife.

Check the seasoning and ladle the stew into shallow bowls. To garnish, spoon some aïoli on to baguette slices and rest them over the stew.

For homemade aïoli, combine the following ingredients in a food processor or blender and blend until creamy: 2 egg yolks, 1 crushed garlic clove, ½ teaspoon sea salt and 1 tablespoon white wine vinegar. Season with pepper. With the motor running, gradually pour 300 ml (½ pint) olive oil through the funnel until the mixture is thick and glossy. Add a little boiling water if it becomes too thick. Transfer to a bowl, cover and refrigerate until required.

chicken & seafood paella

Serves **4**
Preparation time **25 minutes**
Cooking time **45 minutes**

150 ml (¼ pint) **olive oil**
150 g (5 oz) **chorizo**, cut into small pieces
4 boned **chicken thighs**, cut into pieces
300 g (10 oz) **squid rings**
8 large **raw prawns**
1 **red pepper**, deseeded and chopped
4 **garlic cloves**, crushed
1 **onion**, chopped
250 g (8 oz) **paella rice**
1 teaspoon **saffron threads**
450 ml (¾ pint) **chicken stock** or **fish stock** (see pages 16 and 88)
100 g (3½ oz) **peas** or **broad beans**
300 g (10 oz) **fresh mussels**
salt and pepper
lemon or **lime wedges**, to garnish

Heat half the oil in a large paella, sauté or frying pan and gently fry the chorizo for 5 minutes, turning it in the oil. Drain to a plate. Add the chicken thighs to the pan and fry for about 5 minutes until cooked through. Drain to the plate. Cook the squid rings and prawns in the oil, turning the prawns once, until pink. Drain to the plate while cooking the rice.

Add the red pepper, garlic and onion to the pan and fry gently for 5 minutes until softened. Stir in the rice, turning it in the oil for 1 minute. Add the saffron and stock to the pan and bring to the boil. Reduce the heat, cover with a lid or foil and cook gently for about 20 minutes until the rice is cooked through.

Scrub the mussels, scraping off any barnacles and pulling away the beards. Discard any damaged shells or any open ones that don't close when tapped gently with a knife.

Return the chorizo, chicken, squid and prawns to the pan with the peas or beans and mix thoroughly. Scatter the mussels over the top, pushing them down slightly into the rice. Cover and cook for a further 5 minutes or until the mussels have opened. Discard any shells that remain closed. Check the seasoning and serve garnished with lemon or lime wedges.

For pork paella, replace the chicken with 400 g (13 oz) lean belly pork, diced and cooked as above. Replace the squid with 8 fresh scallops with roes and the mussels with the same quantity of small clams.

mussels in tarragon cream sauce

Serves **4**
Preparation time **20 minutes**
Cooking time **15 minutes**

1 kg (2 lb) **fresh mussels**
50 g (2 oz) **butter**
2 **shallots**, finely chopped
2 **garlic cloves**, crushed
1 teaspoon **ground coriander**
2 teaspoons chopped **lemon thyme**
1 tablespoon **plain flour**
1 glass **white wine**, about 150 ml (¼ pint)
2 tablespoons chopped **tarragon**
150 ml (¼ pint) **double cream**
salt and pepper

Scrub the mussels, scraping off any barnacles and pulling away the beards. Discard any damaged shells or any open ones that don't close when tapped firmly with a knife or against the edge of the sink.

Melt the butter in a large saucepan. Add the shallots, garlic, coriander and thyme and fry very gently for 2 minutes. Remove from the heat and stir in the flour to make a thin paste. Gradually beat in the wine, using a whisk or wooden spoon, until smooth.

Return to the heat and cook, stirring, until the sauce is thick and smooth. Stir in the tarragon. Tip in the mussels and cover with a lid. Cook for about 5 minutes, shaking the pan frequently, until the shells have opened.

Drain the mussels to warmed shallow bowls, discarding any that remain closed.

Stir the cream into the sauce and bring to the boil. Season to taste and ladle the sauce over the mussels. Serve with warmed, crusty bread.

For steamed mussels in white wine sauce, prepare the mussels as in the first step. Melt 25 g (1 oz) butter in a large saucepan and fry 1 small onion chopped, 1–2 garlic cloves finely chopped and 1 small leek finely sliced until soft. Add the mussels, 300 ml (½ pint) dry white wine and 150 ml (¼ pint) water, cover and bring to the boil. Cook for 2–5 minutes until the mussels open, then divide into serving bowls. Mix 25 g (1 oz) butter with 15 g (½ oz) plain flour to form a paste. Gradually add to the juices in the pan, stirring to thicken. Bring to the boil, stir in 2 tablespoons chopped parsley, season and pour over the mussels.

spiced fish tagine

Serves **4**
Preparation time **15 minutes**
Cooking time **35 minutes**

625 g (1¼ lb) **halibut steaks**
1 teaspoon **cumin seeds**
1 teaspoon **coriander seeds**
4 tablespoons **olive oil**
1 large **onion**, sliced
3 pared strips of **orange rind**,
   plus 2 tablespoons **juice**
3 **garlic cloves**, sliced
½ teaspoon **saffron threads**
150 ml (¼ pint) **fish stock**
   (see page 88)
50 g (2 oz) **dates**, sliced
25 g (1 oz) **flaked almonds**,
   lightly toasted
salt and pepper

Cut the halibut into chunky pieces, discarding the skin and any bones. Season lightly. Crush the cumin and coriander seeds using a pestle and mortar.

Heat the oil in a large frying pan or sauté pan and gently fry the onion and orange rind for 5 minutes. Add the garlic and crushed spices and fry, stirring, for a further 2–3 minutes.

Add the fish, turning the pieces to coat in the spices. Crumble in the saffron and pour in the stock and orange juice. Scatter with the dates and almonds.

Cover with a lid or foil and cook very gently for 20–25 minutes or until the fish is cooked through. Check the seasoning and serve with steamed couscous.

For spicy swordfish tagine, replace the halibut with the same quantity of swordfish steaks cut into chunks. Add a mild or medium red chilli, deseeded and chopped, with the crushed spices. Use 25 g (1 oz) dried figs and 25 g (1 oz) dried apricots instead of the dates.

spicy fish

Serves **2**
Preparation time **10 minutes,
  plus marinating**
Cooking time **5 minutes**

1 **garlic clove**, peeled
2 **red shallots**, chopped
1 **lemon grass stalk**
½ teaspoon **ground turmeric**
½ teaspoon **ground ginger**
1 **mild red chilli**, deseeded
  and roughly chopped
1 tablespoon **groundnut oil**
2 teaspoon **fish sauce**
300 g (10 oz) boneless
  white fish fillets, cut into
  bite-sized pieces
salt and pepper
1 tablespoon chopped **fresh
  coriander**, to garnish

Put the garlic, shallots, lemon grass, turmeric, ginger, chilli and salt and pepper into a food processor or blender and process until a paste is formed, adding the oil and fish sauce to help the grinding.

Place the fish in a bowl and toss with the spice paste. Cover and refrigerate for 15 minutes.

Thread the pieces of fish on to skewers and arrange on a foil-lined tray. Cook under a preheated hot grill for 4–5 minutes, turning once so that the pieces brown evenly. Serve sprinkled with the coriander.

For Chinese greens to serve as an accompaniment, put 300 g (10 oz) raw shredded Chinese greens in a saucepan of boiling water and cook for 1–2 minutes. Drain and place on warmed serving plates. Heat 1 teaspoon groundnut oil in a small pan and cook $^1/_2$ teaspoon finely chopped garlic briefly. Stir in 1 teaspoon oyster sauce, 1 tablespoon water and $^1/_2$ tablespoon sesame oil, then bring to the boil. Pour over the greens and toss together.

fish pie

Serves **4**
Preparation time **15 minutes**
Cooking time **1 hour 10
minutes**

300 g (10 oz) **raw peeled
prawns**
2 teaspoons **cornflour**
300 g (10 oz) **skinned white
fish**, e.g. **haddock**, cut into
small pieces
2 teaspoons **green
peppercorns in brine**,
rinsed and drained
1 small **fennel bulb**, roughly
chopped
1 small **leek**, roughly chopped
15 g (½ oz) **fresh dill**
15 g (½ oz) **fresh parsley**
100 g (3½ oz) **fresh** or **frozen
peas**
350 g (12 oz) **ready-made** or
homemade cheese sauce
(see page 206)
750 g (1½ lb) **baking
potatoes**, thinly sliced
75 g (3 oz) **Cheddar cheese**,
grated
salt and pepper

Dry the prawns, if frozen and thawed, by patting
between sheets of kitchen paper. Season the cornflour
and use to coat the prawns and white fish. Lightly
crush the peppercorns using a pestle and mortar.

Put the peppercorns in a food processor with the
fennel, leek, dill, parsley and a little salt and blend
until very finely chopped, scraping the mixture down
from the sides of the bowl if necessary. Tip into a
shallow, ovenproof dish.

Scatter the prawns and fish over the fennel mixture
and mix together a little. Scatter the peas on top.

Spoon half the cheese sauce over the filling and
spread roughly with the back of a spoon. Layer up
the potatoes on top, seasoning each layer as you
go. Spoon the remaining sauce over the top,
spreading it in a thin layer. Sprinkle with the cheese.

Bake in a preheated oven, 220°C (425°F), Gas
Mark 7, for 30 minutes until the surface has turned
pale golden. Reduce the oven temperature to 180°C
(350°F), Gas Mark 4, and cook for a further 30–40
minutes until the potatoes are completely tender.
Serve with a tomato salad.

For smoked fish and caper pie, use 625 g (1¼ lb)
smoked pollack, skinned and cut into small chunks
in place of the prawns and white fish. Use 2
tablespoons capers instead of the green peppercorns.

simple seafood curry

Serves **4**
Preparation time **20 minutes**
Cooking time **35 minutes**

40 g (1½ oz) **fresh root
   ginger**, grated
1 teaspoon **ground turmeric**
2 **garlic cloves**, crushed
2 teaspoons **medium curry
   paste**
150 ml (¼ pint) **natural yogurt**
625 g (1¼ lb) **white fish
   fillets**, skinned
2 tablespoons **oil**
1 large **onion**, sliced
1 **cinnamon stick**, halved
2 teaspoons **dark muscovado
   sugar**
2 **bay leaves**
400 g (13 oz) can **chopped
   tomatoes**
300 ml (½ pint) **fish stock**
   or **vegetable stock** (see
   page 190)
500 g (1 lb) **waxy potatoes**,
   cut into small chunks
25 g (1 oz) chopped **fresh
   coriander**
salt and pepper

Mix together the ginger, turmeric, garlic and curry
paste in a bowl. Stir in the yogurt until combined.
Cut the fish into large pieces and add to the bowl,
stirring until coated in the spice mixture.

Heat the oil in a large saucepan and gently fry the
onion, cinnamon, sugar and bay leaves until the onion
is soft. Add the tomatoes, stock and potatoes and bring
to the boil. Cook, uncovered, for about 20 minutes until
the potatoes are tender and the sauce has thickened.

Tip in the fish and spicy yogurt and reduce the heat to
its lowest setting. Cook gently for about 10 minutes or
until the fish is cooked through. Check the seasoning
and stir in the coriander to serve.

For homemade fish stock, melt a knob of butter in a
large saucepan and gently fry off 2 roughly chopped
shallots, 1 small, roughly chopped leek and 1 roughly
chopped celery stick or fennel bulb. Add 1 kg (2 lb)
white fish or shellfish bones, heads and trimmings,
several sprigs of parsley, ½ lemon and 1 teaspoon
peppercorns. Cover with cold water and bring to a
simmer. Cook, uncovered, on the lowest setting for
30 minutes. Strain through a sieve and leave to cool.

sea bass & spicy potatoes

Serves **2**
Preparation time **15 minutes**
Cooking time **1 hour**

500 g (1 lb) **baking potatoes**
3 tablespoons **olive oil**
2 tablespoons **sun-dried
  tomato tapenade**
½ teaspoon **mild chilli
  powder**
2 small whole **sea bass,**
  scaled and gutted
2 tablespoons mixed chopped
  herbs, e.g. **thyme**, **parsley**,
  chervil, **tarragon**
1 **garlic clove**, crushed
2 **bay leaves**
½ **lemon**, sliced
handful of **pitted black olives**
salt and pepper

Cut the potatoes into 1 cm (½ inch) thick slices –
you can peel them first if you wish to, but this isn't
necessary. Cut into chunky chips. Mix 2 tablespoons
of the oil with the tapenade, chilli powder and plenty
of salt. Toss in a bowl with the potatoes until
evenly coated.

Tip the potatoes into a shallow ovenproof dish or
roasting pan and bake in a preheated oven, 200°C
(400°F), Gas Mark 6, for 30 minutes until pale golden,
turning the potatoes once or twice during cooking.

Meanwhile, score the fish several times on each side.
Mix the remaining oil with 1 tablespoon of the herbs,
the garlic and a little salt and pepper. Pack the bay
leaves, lemon slices and remaining herbs into the fish
cavities and lay the fish over the potatoes in the dish,
pushing the potatoes to the edges of the dish.

Brush the garlic and herb oil over the fish and scatter
the olives over the potatoes. Return to the oven for a
further 30 minutes until the fish is cooked through.
Test by piercing the thick end of the fish with a knife;
the flesh should be cooked through to the bone.

For tomato salad to serve as an accompaniment,
slice 2 large tomatoes and arrange on a platter. Slice
½ small red onion and place on top of the tomatoes.
Mix the following dressing ingredients together
thoroughly: 6 tablespoons olive oil, 2 tablespoons
cider vinegar, 1 garlic clove crushed, ½ teaspoon
Dijon mustard and salt and pepper. Drizzle over the
tomatoes and sprinkle over a little chopped parsley.

thai prawn soup

Serves **4**
Preparation time **20 minutes**
Cooking time **20 minutes**

Soup base

5 cm (2in) piece of **galangal**
  or **fresh root ginger**, cut
  into very thin slices
500 ml (1 pint) **coconut milk**
250 ml (8 fl oz) **chicken stock**
  or **vegetable stock** (see
  pages 16 and 190)
2 tablespoons **fish sauce**
6 **kaffir lime leaves**
1–2 tablespoons **green curry**
  paste

Soup

½ bunch **spring onions**,
  chopped
150 g (5 oz) **cup**
  mushrooms, sliced
250 g (8 oz) **broccoli**, finely
  chopped
300 g (10 oz) **raw peeled**
  prawns
1 tablespoon freshly squeezed
  lime juice
4 tablespoons roughly
  chopped **fresh coriander**

To make the soup base, combine the galangal or
ginger, coconut milk, stock, fish sauce, lime leaves
and curry paste in a saucepan and bring to the boil,
then simmer for 10 minutes, stirring occasionally.

Add the spring onions, mushrooms and broccoli
to the hot soup base, then simmer for 5–6 minutes
until the vegetables are cooked but still crunchy.

Add the prawns and simmer for 3–5 minutes until
they are pink and cooked through. Stir in the lime
juice and fresh coriander and serve.

For homemade green curry paste, toast
1 tablespoon coriander seeds and 2 teaspoons
cumin seeds in a dry pan over a medium heat for
2–3 minutes, shaking constantly. Grind the roasted
seeds and 1 teaspoon black peppercorns using a
pestle and mortar until finely ground. Put the ground
spices in a food processor and blend for 5 minutes.
Add 8 roughly chopped large green chillies, 20
chopped shallots, a 5 cm (2 inch) piece fresh root
ginger, chopped, 12 chopped small garlic cloves, 75
g (3 oz) chopped fresh coriander leaves, 6 shredded
kaffir lime leaves, 3 finely chopped lemon grass stalks,
2 teaspoons grated lime rind, 2 teaspoons salt and
2 tablespoons olive oil. Blend for 10 seconds at a
time until you have a smooth paste. Store in the
refrigerator for up to 2 weeks.

spicy prawn & potato sauté

Serves **2**
Preparation time **15 minutes**
Cooking time **25 minutes**

3 tablespoons smooth **mango chutney**
½ teaspoon **hot smoked paprika**
1 tablespoon **lemon** or **lime juice**
4 tablespoons **oil**
400 g (13 oz) **raw peeled prawns**
500 g (1 lb) **baking potatoes**, cut into 1.5 cm (¾ inch) dice
2 **garlic cloves**, crushed
400 g (13 oz) can **chopped tomatoes**
50 g (2 oz) **creamed coconut**, chopped into small pieces
salt and pepper
mustard and cress or **snipped chives**, to garnish

Mix together the mango chutney, paprika and lemon or lime juice in a small bowl.

Heat half the oil in a frying pan or sauté pan and fry the prawns for about 3 minutes, turning once, until pink, then immediately drain them from the pan.

Add the potatoes to the pan with the remaining oil and fry very gently for about 10 minutes, turning frequently, until the potatoes are golden and cooked through. Add the garlic and cook for a further 1 minute.

Add the tomatoes and bring to the boil. Reduce the heat and cook gently until the sauce turns pulpy. Stir in the creamed coconut and mango mixture and cook gently until the coconut has dissolved into the sauce.

Stir in the prawns for a few seconds to heat through. Check the seasoning and serve scattered with mustard and cress or chives.

For curried prawn and sweet potato sauté, replace the paprika with 1–2 teaspoons medium curry paste. Replace the potatoes with the same quantity of sweet potatoes, scrubbed or peeled.

dill & mustard baked salmon

Serves **4**
Preparation time **20 minutes**
Cooking time **55 minutes**

3 tablespoons chopped **dill**
2 tablespoons **grainy mustard**
2 tablespoons **lime juice**
1 tablespoon **caster sugar**
150 ml (¼ pint) **double cream**
2 small **fennel bulbs**, thinly sliced
2 tablespoons **olive oil**
750 g (1½ lb) **salmon fillet**, skinned
4 **hard-boiled eggs**, quartered
250 g (8 oz) **puff pastry**
beaten **egg yolk**, to glaze
salt and pepper

Mix together the dill, mustard, lime juice and sugar in a bowl. Stir in the cream and a little seasoning.

Put the fennel in a 2 litre (3½ pint) shallow, ovenproof dish or pie dish. Drizzle with the oil and bake in a preheated oven, 200°C (400°F), Gas Mark 6, for 20 minutes, turning once or twice during cooking, until softened.

Cut the salmon into 8 chunky pieces and add to the dish with the egg quarters, tucking them between the fennel slices so that all the ingredients are evenly mixed. Spoon the cream mixture over and return to the oven for 15 minutes.

Roll out the pastry on a lightly floured surface and cut out 8 x 6 cm (2½ inch) squares. Brush the tops with egg yolk to glaze and make diagonal markings over the surface of the pastry with the tip of a sharp knife. Sprinkle with pepper.

Place a double thickness of greaseproof paper over the dish of salmon and put the pastry squares on the paper. Bake for 10–15 minutes until the pastry is risen and golden. Slide the pastry squares on to the salmon and serve with a herb salad.

For dill, mustard and salmon pie, replace the lime juice with lemon juice and scatter the salmon with 1 tablespoon capers. Replace the puff pastry with 6 sheets of filo pastry. Place on top of the salmon dish in layers, brushing each layer with melted butter and crumpling slightly. Bake for 20–25 minutes.

feta-stuffed plaice

Serves **4**
Preparation time **20 minutes**
Cooking time **40 minutes**

2 tablespoons chopped **mint**
2 tablespoons chopped
  oregano
25 g (1 oz) **Parma ham**, finely
  chopped
2 **garlic cloves**, crushed
4 **spring onions**, finely
  chopped
200 g (7 oz) **feta cheese**
8 **plaice fillets**, skinned
300 g (10 oz) **courgettes**,
  sliced
4 tablespoons **garlic-infused
  olive oil**
8 **flat mushrooms**
150 g (5 oz) **baby plum
  tomatoes**, halved
1 tablespoon **capers**, rinsed
  and drained
salt and pepper

Put the mint, oregano, ham, garlic and spring onions in a bowl. Crumble in the feta cheese, season with plenty of pepper and mix together well.

Put the fish fillets skinned-side up on the work surface and press the feta mixture down the centres. Roll up loosely and secure with wooden cocktail sticks.

Scatter the courgettes into a shallow, ovenproof dish and drizzle with 1 tablespoon of the oil. Place in a preheated oven, 190°C (375°F), Gas Mark 5, for 15 minutes. Remove from the oven and add the plaice fillets to the dish. Tuck the mushrooms, tomatoes and capers around the fish and season lightly. Drizzle with the remaining oil.

Return to the oven for a further 25 minutes or until the fish is cooked through.

For tomato and garlic bread to serve as an accompaniment, mix together 75 g (3 oz) softened butter, 2 crushed garlic cloves, 3 tablespoons sun-dried tomato paste and a little salt and pepper. Make vertical cuts 2.5 cm (1 inch) apart through a ciabatta loaf, cutting not quite through the base. Push the garlic and tomato paste mixture into the cuts. Wrap in foil and bake in the oven under the fish for 15 minutes. Unwrap the top of the bread and return to the oven for 10 minutes.

plaice with sambal

Serves **4**
Preparation time **30 minutes**
Cooking time **30 minutes**

1 small **lemon grass stalk**
2 **garlic cloves**, crushed
6 tablespoons grated **fresh coconut**
2 **green chillies**, deseeded and finely chopped
4 small whole **plaice**, scaled and gutted
4 tablespoons **oil**

Coconut and tamarind sambal
1 **onion**, finely chopped
1 **garlic clove**, crushed
1 tablespoon **oil**
2 tablespoons grated **fresh coconut**
1 **red chilli**, deseeded and finely chopped
150 ml (¼ pint) **boiling water**
2 tablespoons **dried tamarind pulp**
2 teaspoons **caster sugar**
1 tablespoon **white wine vinegar**
1 tablespoon chopped **fresh coriander**

Finely chop the lemon grass stalk and mix with the garlic, coconut and green chillies. Smear this dry mixture over each plaice, then cover and leave to marinate in the refrigerator for 2 hours or overnight.

Make the coconut and tamarind sambal by gently frying the onion and garlic in the oil in a large frying pan until softened. Add the coconut with the red chilli, stir to coat in the oil and cook for 2–3 minutes. Pour the measurement water over the tamarind pulp in a heatproof bowl and stand for 10 minutes to dissolve.

Strain the juice from the tamarind pulp, mashing as much of the pulp through the sieve as possible. Add this juice to the pan with the sugar and simmer gently for 5 minutes. Add the vinegar, remove from the heat and leave to cool. When cold, stir in the chopped coriander. Turn into a bowl and wipe the pan clean.

Heat the oil in the pan and gently fry the plaice 2 at a time in the hot oil, turning once. After 6–8 minutes, when they are golden brown and cooked, remove from the oil and drain on kitchen paper. Keep warm while cooking the remaining fish. Serve the fish piping hot with the coconut and tamarind sambal.

For perfumed rice to serve as an accompaniment, cook 325 g (11 oz) fragrant long-grain rice in boiling water until tender. Fry 1 bunch spring onions, thinly sliced, in 2 teaspoons oil for 30 seconds. Add the finely grated rind of 1 lime and 4–6 shredded kaffir lime leaves. Stir in the drained rice and a little salt.

haddock & shellfish soup

Serves **4**
Preparation time **15 minutes**
Cooking time **20 minutes**

500 g (1 lb) **undyed smoked
   haddock**
25 g (1 oz) **butter**
1 large **leek**, chopped
2 teaspoons **medium curry
   paste**
1 litre (1¾ pints) **fish stock**
   (see page 88)
50g/2 oz **creamed coconut**,
   chopped
3 **bay leaves**
150 g (5 oz) **French beans**,
   cut into 1 cm (½ inch)
   lengths
3 small **courgettes**, chopped
250 g (8 oz) **cooked mixed
   seafood**, e.g. **prawns,
   mussels, squid rings**,
   thawed if frozen
100 ml (3½ fl oz) **single
   cream**
4 tablespoons finely chopped
   parsley
salt and pepper

Cut the haddock into small pieces, discarding the skin
and any bones.

Melt the butter in a large saucepan and gently fry the
leek for 3 minutes to soften. Add the curry paste, stock
and creamed coconut and bring almost to the boil.
Reduce the heat and simmer gently, covered, for
10 minutes until the leek is soft.

Stir in the bay leaves, beans and courgettes and
cook for 2 minutes to soften slightly. Add the smoked
haddock and mixed seafood, 3 tablespoons of the
cream and the parsley and cook very gently for
5 minutes until the haddock flakes easily.

Season to taste and spoon into serving bowls. Serve
swirled with the remaining cream.

For smoked salmon and mangetout soup, replace
the haddock with 500 g (1 lb) lightly smoked salmon
and cook as above. Replace the French beans with
the same quantity of mangetout.

mediterranean roasted fish

Serves **4**
Preparation time **15 minutes**
Cooking time **40 minutes**

5 tablespoons **olive oil**
2 **shallots**, thinly sliced
75 g (3 oz) **pancetta**,
    chopped
50 g (2 oz) **pine nuts**
2 teaspoons chopped
    rosemary, plus several
    extra sprigs
1 thick slice **white bread**,
    made into breadcrumbs
50 g (2 oz) can **anchovies**,
    drained and chopped
2 **red onions**, thinly sliced
6 **tomatoes**, cut into wedges
2 **haddock fillets**, each about
    300 g (10 oz), skinned
salt and pepper

Heat 2 tablespoons of the oil in a large roasting pan
and fry the shallots and pancetta, stirring frequently,
until beginning to colour. Add the pine nuts and
chopped rosemary with a little pepper and fry
for a further 2 minutes. Drain to a bowl, add
the breadcrumbs and anchovies and mix well.

Add the onions to the pan and fry for 5 minutes
until slightly softened. Stir in the tomato wedges
and remove from the heat. Push to the edges of
the pan to leave a space for the fish in the centre.

Check the fish for any stray bones and place one fillet
in the pan. Pack the stuffing mixture on top, pressing
it firmly on to the fish with your hands. Lay the second
fillet on top, skinned-side down, and season with a
little salt and pepper.

Drizzle with the remaining oil and place in a preheated
oven, 180°C (350°F), Gas Mark 4, for 30 minutes until
the fish is cooked through. Test by piercing a thick area
with a knife.

For spinach and walnut salad to serve as an
accompaniment, heat 1 tablespoon clear honey in a
small frying pan, add 125 g (4 oz) walnuts and stir-fry
over a medium heat for 2–3 minutes until glazed.
Meanwhile, blanch 250 g (8 oz) green beans in lightly
salted boiling water for 3 minutes and drain. Place in a
large bowl with 200 g (7 oz) baby spinach. Whisk the
following dressing ingredients together and season
with salt and pepper: 4 tablespoons walnut oil, 2
tablespoons olive oil and 1–2 tablespoons sherry
vinegar. Pour over the leaves and scatter the walnuts.

seafood lemon grass crumble

Serves **4**
Preparation time **20 minutes**
Cooking time **40 minutes**

500 g (1 lb) **swordfish
steaks**
200 g (7 oz) **raw peeled
prawns**
250 g (8 oz) **mascarpone
cheese**
4 tablespoons **white wine**
1 **lemon grass stalk**
150 g (5 oz) **plain flour**
75 g (3 oz) **butter**, cut into
pieces
4 tablespoons chopped **dill**
4 tablespoons freshly grated
Parmesan cheese
salt and pepper

Cut the swordfish into large chunks, discarding any skin and bones, and scatter in a 1.5 litre (2½ pint) ovenproof dish or pie dish. Add the prawns and season with salt and pepper.

Beat the mascarpone in a bowl to soften. Stir in the wine and spoon over the fish.

Chop the lemon grass as finely as possible and process in a blender or food processor with the flour and butter until the mixture resembles fine breadcrumbs. Add the dill and pulse very briefly to mix.

Tip the mixture over the fish and sprinkle with the Parmesan. Bake in a preheated oven, 190°C (375°F), Gas Mark 5, for about 35–40 minutes until the topping is pale golden. Serve with a green salad.

For seafood puff pastry pie, omit the Parmesan cheese and replace the lemon grass crumble with 500 g (1 lb) puff pastry. Roll out the pastry on a lightly floured surface, then place on top of the fish in the dish. Brush the top with egg yolk to glaze, then sprinkle with pepper. Bake the pie in a preheated oven, 220°C (425°F), Gas Mark 7, for 15 minutes then reduce the heat to 180°C (350°F), Gas Mark 4, and bake for a further 15–20 minutes until golden.

clam & potato chowder

Serves **4**
Preparation time **15 minutes**
Cooking time **30 minutes**

1 kg (2 lb) small **fresh clams**
25 g (1 oz) **butter**
2 **onions**, chopped
150 ml (¼ pint) **white wine**
1.2 litres (2 pints) **fish stock**
   or **chicken stock** (see pages
   88 and 16)
½ teaspoon **medium curry
   paste**
¼ teaspoon **ground turmeric**
500 g (1 lb) **floury potatoes,**
   diced
150 g (5 oz) **watercress,**
   tough stalks removed
plenty of freshly grated
   nutmeg
squeeze of **lemon juice**
salt and pepper

Rinse and check over the clams, discarding any damaged shells or any open ones that don't close when tapped with a knife. Transfer to a bowl.

Melt the butter in a large saucepan and gently fry the onions for 6–8 minutes until soft. Add the wine and bring to the boil. Tip in the clams and cover with a lid. Cook for about 5 minutes until the clams have opened, shaking the pan several times during cooking.

Once the shells are all opened, remove from the heat and tip into a colander set over a large bowl to catch the juices. When cool enough to handle, remove the clams from the shells and discard the shells. Reserve the clams and tip the cooking juices back into the pan.

Add the stock, curry paste, turmeric and potatoes to the saucepan and bring to the boil. Reduce the heat, cover and simmer for 10–15 minutes until the potatoes are tender.

Return the clams to the pan with the watercress, nutmeg and lemon juice and heat through gently for 2 minutes. Use a stick blender to lightly blend the chowder without completely puréeing it. Season with salt and pepper to taste.

For mussel, spinach and potato chowder, replace the clams with the same quantity of mussels and prepare as above. Replace the watercress with the same quantity of baby spinach.

oven-steamed fish with greens

Serves **2**
Preparation time **15 minutes**
Cooking time **25 minutes**

15 g (½ oz) **fresh root ginger**
¼ teaspoon **crushed dried chillies**
1 **garlic clove**, thinly sliced
2 tablespoons **rice wine vinegar**
2 chunky **cod fillets**, each 150g–200 g (5–7 oz), skinned
150 ml (¼ pint) hot **fish stock** (see page 88)
½ **cucumber**
2 tablespoons **light soy sauce**
2 tablespoons **oyster sauce**
1 tablespoon **caster sugar**
½ bunch **spring onions**, cut into 2.5 cm (1 inch) lengths
25 g (1 oz) **fresh coriander**, roughly chopped
200 g (7 oz) **ready-cooked rice**

Peel and slice the ginger as finely as possible. Cut across into thin shreds and mix with the crushed chillies, garlic and 1 teaspoon of the vinegar. Spoon over the pieces of cod, rubbing it in gently.

Lightly oil a wire rack and position over a small roasting pan. Pour the stock into the pan and place the cod fillets on the rack. Cover with foil and carefully transfer to a preheated oven, 180°C (350°F), Gas Mark 4, for 20 minutes or until cooked through.

Meanwhile, peel the cucumber, cut in half and scoop out the seeds. Cut the flesh into small, chip-sized pieces. Mix together the soy sauce, oyster sauce, sugar and remaining vinegar in a small bowl.

Remove the fish from the pan and keep warm. Drain off the juices from the pan and reserve. Add the cucumber, spring onions, coriander and rice to the pan and heat through, stirring, for about 5 minutes until hot, stirring in enough of the reserved juices to make the rice slightly moist.

Pile on to serving plates, top with the fish and serve with the sauce spooned over.

For oven-steamed chicken with greens, replace the fish with 4 small skinned chicken breast fillets. Use chicken stock (see page 16) instead of the fish stock. Make several deep scores in the chicken fillets, then cook as per the second step but for 30–40 minutes. Replace the oyster sauce with the same quantity of hoisin sauce.

salt cod with potatoes

Serves **4**
Preparation time **15 minutes**,
  plus soaking
Cooking time **35 minutes**

500 g (1 lb) **salt cod**
4 tablespoons **olive oil**
1 **onion**, finely chopped
3 **garlic cloves**, crushed
600 ml (1 pint) **fish stock**
  (see page 88)
½ teaspoon **saffron threads**
750 g (1½ lb) **floury**
  potatoes, cut into small
  chunks
500 g (1 lb) **cherry plum**
  tomatoes, roughly chopped
4 tablespoons chopped
  parsley
salt and pepper

Put the salt cod in a bowl, cover with plenty of cold water and leave to soak for 1–2 days, changing the water twice daily. Drain the cod and cut into small chunks, discarding any skin and bones.

Heat the oil in a large saucepan and gently fry the onion for 5 minutes until softened. Add the garlic and cook for 1 minute. Add the stock and crumble in the saffron. Bring to the boil, then reduce the heat to a gentle simmer.

Add the salt cod and potatoes and cover with a lid. Cook gently for about 20 minutes until the fish and potatoes are very tender.

Stir in the tomatoes and parsley and then cook for 5 minutes until the tomatoes have softened. Season to taste (you might not need any salt, depending on the saltiness of the fish). Ladle into shallow bowls and serve with warm bread.

For smoked trout with potatoes, replace the salt cod with 300 g (10 oz) smoked trout. Cut into chunks, but don't soak in the first step. Add to the saucepan once the potatoes are cooked, along with 2 tablespoons capers, rinsed and drained, and 2 teaspoons green peppercorns in brine, rinsed, drained and crushed.

hot & sour soup

Serves **4**
Preparation time **10 minutes**
Cooking time **10 minutes**

600 ml (1 pint) **fish stock**
  (see page 88)
4 **kaffir lime leaves**
4 slices of **fresh root ginger**
1 **red chilli**, deseeded and
  sliced
1 **lemon grass stalk**
125 g (4 oz) **mushrooms,**
  sliced
100 g (3½ oz) **dried rice**
  noodles
75 g (3 oz) **baby spinach**
125 g (4 oz) **cooked peeled**
  tiger prawns
2 tablespoons **lemon juice**
pepper

Put the stock, lime leaves, ginger, chilli and lemon grass in a large saucepan. Cover and bring to the boil. Add the mushrooms, reduce the heat and simmer for 2 minutes.

Break the noodles into short lengths, drop into the soup and simmer for 3 minutes. Add the spinach and prawns and simmer for 2 minutes until the prawns are heated through. Add the lemon juice. Remove and discard the lemon grass stalk and season with pepper before serving.

For wholemeal soda bread to serve as an accompaniment, stir 250 g (8 oz) plain white flour, 1 teaspoon bicarbonate of soda, 2 teaspoons cream of tartar and 2 teaspoons salt into a large bowl. Stir in 375 g (12 oz) wholemeal flour, 300 ml (½ pint) milk and 4 tablespoons water and mix to a soft dough. Turn out on to a floured surface, knead lightly, then shape into a large round about 5 cm (2 inches) thick. Put on a floured baking sheet, cut a deep cross in the top and sprinkle with flour. Bake in a preheated oven, 220°C (425°F), Gas Mark 7, for 25–30 minutes.

mackerel & cider vichyssoise

Serves **3–4 as a main course, 8 as a starter**
Preparation time **15 minutes**
Cooking time **30 minutes**

625 g (1¼ lb) **leeks**
50 g (2 oz) **butter**
625 g (1¼ lb) **new potatoes,** diced
600 ml (1 pint) **strong cider**
600 ml (1 pint) **fish stock** (see page 88)
2 teaspoons **Dijon mustard**
300 g (10 oz) **smoked mackerel fillets**
5 tablespoons chopped **chives**
plenty of freshly ground **nutmeg**
200 g (7 oz) **crème fraîche**
salt and pepper
chive sprigs, to garnish

Trim the leeks and chop, keeping the white and green parts separate. Melt the butter in a large saucepan and gently fry the white parts and half the green parts for 5 minutes. Add the potatoes, then stir in the cider, stock and mustard and bring almost to the boil. Reduce the heat and cook gently for 20 minutes until the potatoes are soft but still holding their shape.

Flake the smoked mackerel into small pieces, discarding any skin and stray bones. Add to the pan with the chopped chives, nutmeg and remaining green leeks. Simmer gently for 5 minutes.

Stir in half the crème fraîche and season to taste with salt and pepper. Spoon into bowls, top with the remaining crème fraîche and garnish with chive sprigs.

For trout and white wine vichyssoise, replace the cider with 300 ml (½ pint) dry white wine and add an extra 300 ml (½ pint) fish stock. Instead of the mackerel, use 500 g (1 lb) fresh skinned and boned trout and flake and cook as above. Replace the crème fraiche with 150 ml (¼ pint) single cream.

meat

lamb with artichokes & gremolata

Serves **4**
Preparation time **20 minutes**
Cooking time **25 minutes**

500 g (1 lb) **lamb neck fillet**
2 teaspoons **plain flour**
4 tablespoons **olive oil**
1 **onion**, finely chopped
1 **celery stick**, thinly sliced
150 ml (¼ pint) **chicken stock**
  or **vegetable stock**
  (see pages 16 and 190)
2 **garlic cloves**, finely
  chopped
finely grated **rind** of 1 **lemon**
4 tablespoons chopped
  parsley
150 g (5 oz) shop-bought or
  homemade **roasted
  artichokes**, thinly sliced
4 tablespoons **double cream**
salt and pepper

Trim any excess fat from the lamb and cut into thin slices. Season the flour with salt and pepper and use to coat the lamb. Heat half the oil in a large frying pan and fry the lamb, half at a time, until browned, draining each batch to a plate.

Gently fry the onion and celery in the remaining oil for 5 minutes until softened. Return the lamb to the pan and stir in the stock. Bring to the boil, then reduce the heat and simmer very gently for about 8 minutes until the lamb is cooked through.

Meanwhile, make the gremolata by mixing together the garlic, lemon rind and parsley.

Add the artichokes and cream to the pan and heat through for 2 minutes. Check the seasoning and serve sprinkled with the gremolata.

For home-roasted artichokes, thoroughly drain and slice a can of artichoke hearts. Drizzle with olive oil, sprinkle with dried oregano and seasoning and roast in a preheated oven, 200°C (400°F), Gas Mark 6, for 20–25 minutes.

moroccan lamb

Serves **2**
Preparation time **15 minutes,
plus marinating**
Cooking time **1½ hours**

1 teaspoon **ground ginger**
1 teaspoon **ground cumin**
1 teaspoon **ground paprika**
1 **cinnamon stick**
50 ml (2 fl oz) **orange juice**
250 g (8 oz) **lean lamb**, cut
  into 5 cm (2 inch) cubes
125 g (4 oz) **button onions** or
  shallots, unpeeled
1 tablespoon **olive oil**
1 **garlic clove**, crushed
2 teaspoons **plain flour**
2 teaspoons **tomato purée**
125 ml (4 fl oz) **lamb stock**
  (see page 140)
3 tablespoons **sherry**
50 g (2 oz) ready-to-eat **dried
  apricots**
300 g (10 oz) **canned
  chickpeas**, rinsed and
  drained
salt and pepper

Put the spices in a large bowl and pour the orange juice over them. Add the lamb and mix well, then cover and leave in a cool place for at least 1 hour, or preferably overnight in the refrigerator.

Put the onions or shallots in a heatproof bowl and cover with boiling water. Leave for 2 minutes. Drain and refresh under cold water, then peel.

Heat the oil in a large, flameproof casserole. Remove the lamb from the marinade and pat dry with kitchen paper. Brown over a high heat until golden all over. Using a slotted spoon, remove the lamb and set aside. Reduce the heat slightly and, adding a little more oil if necessary, cook the onions or shallots and garlic for 3 minutes or until just beginning to brown. Return the meat to the pan and stir in the flour and tomato purée. Cook for 1 minute.

Add the marinade to the pan with the stock, sherry and seasoning. Bring to the boil, then reduce the heat, cover and place in a preheated oven, 180°C (350°F), Gas Mark 4, for 1 hour. Add the apricots and chickpeas and cook for a further 15 minutes. Serve with couscous cooked according to the packet instructions.

For Moroccan chicken, replace the lamb with the same quantity of chicken breast meat, cut into cubes and cook as above. Replace the apricots with the same quantity of raisins.

meatballs with tomato sauce

Serves **4**
Preparation time **25 minutes**
Cooking time **30 minutes**

500 g (1 lb) **lean minced beef**
3 **garlic cloves**, crushed
2 **small onions**, finely chopped
25 g (1 oz) **breadcrumbs**
40 g (1½ oz) freshly grated **Parmesan cheese**
6 tablespoons **olive oil**
100 ml (3½ fl oz) **red wine**
2 x 400 g (13 oz) cans **chopped tomatoes**
1 teaspoon **caster sugar**
3 tablespoons **sun-dried tomato paste**
75 g (3 oz) **pitted Italian black olives**, roughly chopped
4 tablespoons roughly chopped **oregano**
125 g (4 oz) **mozzarella cheese**, thinly sliced
salt and pepper

Put the beef in a bowl with half the crushed garlic and half the onion, the breadcrumbs and 25 g (1 oz) of the Parmesan. Season and use your hands to thoroughly blend the ingredients together. Shape into small balls, about 2.5 cm (1 inch) in diameter.

Heat half the oil in a large frying pan or sauté pan and fry the meatballs, shaking the pan frequently, for about 10 minutes until browned. Drain.

Add the remaining oil and onion to the pan and fry until softened. Add the wine and let the mixture bubble until the wine has almost evaporated. Stir in the remaining garlic, the tomatoes, sugar, tomato paste and a little seasoning. Bring to the boil and let the mixture bubble until slightly thickened.

Stir in the olives, all but 1 tablespoon of the oregano and the meatballs. Cook gently for a further 5 minutes.

Arrange the mozzarella slices over the top and scatter with the remaining oregano and Parmesan. Season with black pepper and cook under the grill until the cheese starts to melt. Serve in shallow bowls with warmed, crusty bread.

For Greek-style meatballs, use 500 g (1 lb) lean minced lamb instead of the beef. Replace the olives with 50 g (2 oz) pine nuts. Before adding them to the pan in the fourth step, dry-fry in a small frying pan over a medium heat for 3–5 minutes until lightly browned, shaking constantly.

spicy sausage cassoulet

Serves **2**
Preparation time **15 minutes**
Cooking time **35 minutes**

3 tablespoons **olive oil**
1 **red onion**, finely chopped
1 **garlic clove**, crushed
1 **red pepper**, deseeded and
roughly chopped
2 **celery sticks**, roughly
chopped
200 g (7 oz) can **chopped
tomatoes**
125 ml (4 fl oz) **chicken stock**
(see page 16)
2 teaspoons **dark soy sauce**
1 teaspoon **Dijon mustard**
400 g (13 oz) can **black-eyed
beans**, rinsed and drained
125 g (4 oz) **smoked pork
sausage**, roughly chopped
50 g (2 oz) **fresh
breadcrumbs**
25 g (1 oz) freshly grated
Parmesan cheese
2 tablespoons chopped
parsley

Heat 1 tablespoon of the oil in a frying pan or small
sauté pan. Add the onion, garlic, red pepper and celery
and cook over a low heat, stirring occasionally, for
3–4 minutes.

Add the tomatoes, stock and soy sauce. Bring to the
boil, then reduce the heat and simmer for about 15
minutes, or until the sauce begins to thicken. Add the
mustard, beans and sausage and continue to cook for
a further 10 minutes.

Mix the breadcrumbs, Parmesan and parsley together
and sprinkle over the sausage mixture. Drizzle with the
remaining oil. Place under a preheated moderate–hot
grill for 2–3 minutes or until golden brown.

For mixed leaf and pomegranate salad to serve as
an accompaniment, put 1½ tablespoons raspberry
vinegar and 1 tablespoon olive oil with a little salt
and pepper in a salad bowl and mix lightly. Cut ½
pomegranate into large pieces and flex the skin so
that the small seeds fall out. Add the seeds to the
salad bowl. Break 50 g (2 oz) mixed salad leaves into
bite-sized pieces and add to the salad bowl, tossing
all the ingredients in the salad dressing.

beef, pumpkin & ginger stew

Serves **6**
Preparation time **20 minutes**
Cooking time 1½ **hours**

2 tablespoons **plain flour**
750 g (1½ lb) **lean stewing beef**, diced
25 g (1 oz) **butter**
3 tablespoons **oil**
1 **onion**, chopped
2 **carrots**, sliced
2 **parsnips**, sliced
3 **bay leaves**
several **thyme sprigs**
2 tablespoons **tomato purée**
625 g (1¼ lb) **pumpkin**, peeled, deseeded and cut into small chunks
1 tablespoon **dark muscovado sugar**
50 g (2 oz) **fresh root ginger**, finely chopped
small handful of **parsley**, chopped, plus extra to garnish
salt and pepper

Season the flour with salt and pepper and use to coat the beef. Melt the butter with the oil in a large saucepan and fry the meat in 2 batches until browned, draining with a slotted spoon.

Add the onion, carrots and parsnips to the saucepan and fry gently for 5 minutes.

Return the meat to the pan and add the herbs and tomato purée. Add just enough water to cover the ingredients and bring slowly to the boil. Reduce the heat to its lowest setting, cover with a lid and simmer very gently for 45 minutes.

Add the pumpkin, sugar, ginger and parsley and cook for a further 30 minutes until the pumpkin is soft and the meat is tender. Check the seasoning and serve scattered with extra parsley.

For beef, sweet potato and horseradish stew,
replace the pumpkin with 500 g (1 lb) sweet potato, cut into chunks and cooked as above. Replace the ginger with 3 tablespoons hot horseradish sauce.

asian lamb burgers

Serves **4**
Preparation time **20 minutes**
Cooking time **30 minutes**

2 **garlic cloves**, crushed
1 **lemon grass stalk**, finely
chopped
25 g (1 oz) **fresh root ginger**,
grated
large handful of **fresh
coriander**, roughly chopped
1 **hot red chilli**, deseeded and
thinly sliced
500 g (1 lb) **lean minced
lamb**
2 tablespoons **oil**
1 small **cucumber**
1 bunch **spring onions**
200 g (7 oz) **pak choi**
3 tablespoons **light
muscovado sugar**
finely grated **rind** of 2 **limes**,
plus 4 tablespoons **juice**
2 tablespoon **fish sauce**
50 g (2 oz) **roasted peanuts**
salt

Blend the garlic, lemon grass, ginger, coriander, chilli
and a little salt in a food processor to make a thick
paste. Add the lamb and blend until mixed. Tip out on
to the work surface and divide the mixture into 4 pieces.
Roll each into a ball and flatten into a burger shape.

Heat the oil in a sturdy roasting pan and fry the
burgers on both sides to sear. Transfer to a preheated
oven, 200°C (400°F), Gas Mark 6, and cook,
uncovered, for 25 minutes until the burgers are
cooked through.

Meanwhile, peel the cucumber and cut in half
lengthways. Scoop out the seeds with a teaspoon
and discard. Cut the cucumber into thin, diagonal
slices. Slice the spring onions diagonally. Roughly
shred the pak choi, keeping the white parts separate
from the green.

Using a large metal spoon, drain off all but about
2 tablespoons fat from the roasting pan. Arrange all
the vegetables except the green parts of the pak choi
around the meat and toss them gently in the pan
juices. Return to the oven, uncovered, for 5 minutes.

Mix together the sugar, lime rind and juice and fish
sauce. Scatter the pak choi greens and peanuts into
the roasting pan and drizzle with half the dressing.
Toss the salad ingredients together gently. Transfer
the lamb and salad to serving plates and drizzle with
the remaining dressing.

For chicken burgers, use minced chicken instead of
the lamb. Replace the pak choi with shredded spring
greens and peanuts with salted cashews.

greek lamb with tzatziki toasts

Serves **4**
Preparation time **15 minutes**
Cooking time **1½ hours**

750 g (1½ lb) **lamb chump chops**
2 teaspoons **dried oregano**
3 **garlic cloves**, crushed
4 tablespoons **olive oil**
1 medium **aubergine**, about 300 g (10 oz), diced
2 **red onions**, sliced
200 ml (7 fl oz) **white** or **red wine**
400 g (13 oz) can **chopped tomatoes**
2 tablespoons **clear honey**
8 **kalamata olives**
8 thin slices **French stick**
200 g (7 oz) **tzatziki**
salt and pepper

Cut the lamb into large pieces, discarding any excess fat. Mix the oregano with the garlic and a little seasoning and rub into the lamb.

Heat half the oil in a large saucepan or sauté pan and fry the lamb in batches until browned. Drain to a plate.

Add the aubergine to the pan with the onions and remaining oil and cook very gently, stirring frequently, for about 10 minutes until softened and lightly browned. Return the meat to the pan with the wine, tomatoes, honey, olives and seasoning. Cover with a lid and cook on the lowest setting for about 1¼ hours or until the lamb is very tender. Lightly toast the bread and spoon the tzatziki on top.

Check the stew for seasoning and turn into shallow bowls. Serve with the toasts on the side.

For homemade tzatziki, coarsely grate a 5 cm (2 inch) piece peeled cucumber and pat dry between several sheets of kitchen paper. In a bowl, mix with 200 g (7 oz) natural yogurt, 1 tablespoon finely chopped mint, 1 crushed garlic clove and seasoning.

steak & ale casserole

Serves **5–6**
Preparation time **20 minutes**
Cooking time 1¾ **hours**

2 tablespoons **plain flour**
1 kg (2 lb) **braising steak**, cut
  into chunks
25 g (1 oz) **butter**
1 tablespoon **oil**
2 **onions**, chopped
2 **celery sticks**, sliced
several **thyme sprigs**
2 **bay leaves**
400 ml (14 fl oz) **strong ale**
300 ml (½ pint) **beef stock**
  (see page 138)
2 tablespoons **black treacle**
500 g (1 lb) **parsnips**, peeled
  and cut into wedges
salt and pepper

Season the flour with salt and pepper and use to coat the beef. Melt the butter with the oil in a large, flameproof casserole and fry the beef in batches until deep brown. Drain with a slotted spoon while cooking the remainder.

Add the onions and celery and fry gently for 5 minutes. Return the beef to the pan and add the herbs, ale, stock and treacle. Bring just to the boil, then reduce the heat and cover with a lid. Bake in a preheated oven, 160°C (325°F), Gas Mark 3, for 1 hour.

Add the parsnips to the dish and return to the oven for a further 30 minutes or until the beef and parsnips are tender. Check the seasoning and serve.

For potato champ to serve as an accompaniment, cook 1.5 kg (3 lb) scrubbed potatoes in a large saucepan of salted boiling water for 20 minutes. Peel away the skins, then return to the pan and mash. Beat in 150 ml (¼ pint) milk, 3–4 finely chopped spring onions and 50 g (2 oz) butter. Season with salt and pepper and then serve.

chilli & pancetta marrow cups

Serves **4**
Preparation time **20 minutes**
Cooking time **45 minutes**

150 g (5 oz) **ciabatta**
100 g (3½ oz) **pine nuts**
1.25 kg (2½ lb) **marrow**
50 g (2 oz) **butter**
4 tablespoons **olive oil**
75 g (3 oz) **pancetta**, cubed
3 **garlic cloves**, crushed
1 **mild red chilli**, deseeded
  and sliced
½ teaspoon **hot smoked
  paprika**
2 teaspoons chopped **thyme
  leaves**
small handful **curly parsley**,
  chopped
salt

Crumble the ciabatta into small pieces and spread out on a foil-lined grill rack. Scatter with the pine nuts and grill lightly until toasted.

Peel the marrow and cut across into 4 even-sized lengths, trimming off the ends. Using a dessertspoon, scoop out the seeds, leaving a small base in each, to make cups.

Melt the butter with 2 tablespoons of the oil in a small roasting pan and gently fry the pancetta for about 5 minutes until beginning to crisp and colour. Add the garlic, chilli and paprika and cook for a further 1 minute. Drain to a large bowl, leaving a little of the spicy oil in the pan.

Off the heat, put the marrow cups in the pan, turning them in the oil. Place upright and brush the centres with more of the spicy oil in the pan. Season with salt and bake in a preheated oven, 200°C (400°F), Gas Mark 6, for 25 minutes or until tender.

Toss the pine nuts and ciabatta with the pancetta mixture and herbs and divide between the cups. Drizzle with the remaining oil and return to the oven for a further 15 minutes.

For sun-dried tomato pumpkin cups, replace the pancetta with 50 g (2 oz) finely chopped sun-dried tomatoes and fry off in the same way. Replace the marrow with small, single-portion-sized pumpkins. Slice off the tops and scoop out the seeds. Brush the spicy oil on the insides and bake for 50 minutes or until soft.

chilli con carne

Serves **2**
Preparation time **15 minutes**
Cooking time **45 minutes**

2 tablespoon **olive oil**
1 **red onion**, finely chopped
3 **garlic cloves**, finely
 chopped
250 g (8 oz) **lean minced
 beef**
½ teaspoon **ground cumin**
1 small **red pepper**, deseeded
 and diced
400 g (13 oz) can **chopped
 tomatoes**
1 tablespoon **tomato purée**
2 teaspoons **mild chilli
 powder**
200 ml (7 fl oz) **beef stock**
400 g (13 oz) can **red kidney
 beans**, rinsed and drained
salt and pepper

Heat the oil in a saucepan. Add the onion and garlic and cook for 5 minutes or until beginning to soften. Add the mince and cumin and cook for a further 5–6 minutes or until browned all over.

Stir in the red pepper, tomatoes, tomato purée, chilli powder and stock and bring to the boil. Reduce the heat and simmer gently for 30 minutes.

Add the beans and cook for a further 5 minutes. Season to taste and serve with brown rice, cooked according to the packet instructions.

For homemade beef stock, put 750g (1½ lb) raw or cooked beef bones in a large, heavy-based saucepan with a large, unpeeled and halved onion, 2 carrots and 2 celery sticks, roughly chopped, 1 teaspoon peppercorns and several bay leaves and thyme sprigs. Cover with cold water and heat until simmering. Reduce the heat to its lowest setting and cook very gently, uncovered, for 3–4 hours. Strain through a sieve and leave to cool. Store for up to a week in the refrigerator or freezer.

lamb & red rice pilaf

Serves **3–4**
Preparation time **20 minutes**
Cooking time **1 hour**
10 minutes

2 teaspoons **cumin seeds**
2 teaspoons **coriander seeds**
10 **cardamom pods**
3 tablespoons **olive oil**
500 g (1 lb) **shoulder of lamb**, diced
2 **red onions**, sliced
25 g (1 oz) **fresh root ginger**, grated
2 **garlic cloves**, crushed
½ teaspoon **ground turmeric**
200 g (7 oz) **red rice**
600 ml (1 pint) **lamb stock** or **chicken stock** (see page 16)
40 g (1½ oz) **pine nuts**
75 g (3 oz) ready-to-eat **dried apricots**, thinly sliced
50 g (2 oz) **rocket**
salt and pepper

Grind the cumin, coriander and cardamom pods using a pestle and mortar until the cardamom pods have opened to release the seeds. Discard the shells.

Heat the oil in a small, sturdy roasting pan and fry the spices for 30 seconds. Add the lamb and onions and toss with the spices. Transfer to a preheated oven, 180°C (350°F), Gas Mark 4, and cook for 40 minutes until the lamb and onions are browned.

Return to the hob and stir in the ginger, garlic, turmeric and rice. Add the stock and bring to the boil. Cover with a lid or foil and cook over the lowest setting for about 30 minutes until the rice is tender and the stock has been absorbed.

Stir in the pine nuts and apricots and season to taste. Scatter with the rocket and fold in very lightly. Pile on to serving plates and serve immediately.

For homemade lamb stock, put 750 g (1½ lb) roasted lamb bones and meat scraps in a large, heavy-based saucepan with 1 large onion, roughly chopped, 2 large carrots and 2 celery sticks, both roughly sliced, 1 teaspoon black peppercorns and several bay leaves and thyme sprigs. Just cover with cold water and bring slowly to the boil. Reduce the heat and simmer for 3 hours, skimming the surface if necessary. Strain through a sieve and leave to cool. Store for up to a week in the refrigerator or freezer.

meaty boston beans

Serves **4–6**

Preparation time **15 minutes,
plus overnight soaking**

Cooking time **2 hours**

300 g (10 oz) **haricot beans**

15 g (½ oz) **butter**

200 g (7 oz) **smoked bacon
lardons**

375 g (12 oz) **lean diced
pork**

1 **onion**, chopped

1 tablespoon chopped **thyme
or rosemary**

400 g (13 oz) can **chopped
tomatoes**

3 tablespoons **black treacle**

2 tablespoons **tomato purée**

2 tablespoons **grainy
mustard**

1 tablespoon **Worcestershire
sauce**

salt and pepper

Put the beans in a bowl, cover with cold water and leave to soak overnight.

Drain the beans and put in a flameproof casserole. Cover with water and bring to the boil. Reduce the heat and simmer gently for 15–20 minutes or until the beans have softened slightly. Test by removing a few on a fork and squeezing them gently – they should give a little. Drain the beans.

Wipe out the dish and melt the butter. Add the bacon and pork and fry gently for 10 minutes until beginning to brown. Add the onion and cook for a further 5 minutes.

Stir in the drained beans, thyme or rosemary and tomatoes. Add enough water to just cover the ingredients and bring to the boil. Cover with a lid and transfer to a preheated oven, 150°C (300°F), Gas Mark 2. Cook for about 1 hour or until the beans are very tender.

Mix together the treacle, tomato purée, mustard, Worcestershire sauce and seasoning. Stir into the beans and return to the oven for a further 30 minutes.

For veggie Boston beans, replace the haricot beans with the same quantity of butter beans and soak and drain as above. Replace the bacon and pork with 12 vegetarian sausages and fry off before the onion in the third step until lightly browned. Remove from the pan and set aside. Add the onion and continue as above. Add the veggie sausages in the final stage before the sauce and cook for 30 minutes.

beef & flat noodle soup

Serves **4–6**
Preparation time **30 minutes**
Cooking time **2 hours**

1 tablespoon **vegetable oil**
500 g (1 lb) **braising beef**
1.8 litres (3 pints) **beef stock** (see page 138)
4 **star anise**
1 **cinnamon stick**
1 teaspoon **black peppercorns**
4 **shallots**, thinly sliced
4 **garlic cloves**, crushed
7 cm (3 inch) piece of **fresh root ginger**, finely sliced
300 g (10 oz) **flat rice noodles**
125 g (4 oz) **bean sprouts**
6 **spring onions**, thinly sliced
handful of **fresh coriander**
250 g (8 oz) **beef fillet**, sliced
2 tablespoons **fish sauce**
salt and pepper
hot red chillies, to garnish

nuoc cham sauce
2 **red chillies**, chopped
1 **garlic clove**, chopped
1½ tablespoons **caster sugar**
1 tablespoon **lime juice**
1 tablespoon **rice wine vinegar**
3 tablespoons **fish sauce**

Heat the oil in a large saucepan or casserole and sear the beef on all sides until thoroughly brown.

Add the stock, star anise, cinnamon, black peppercorns, half the shallots, the garlic and ginger. Bring to the boil, removing any scum. Reduce the heat, cover the pan with a lid and simmer very gently for about 1½ hours or until the beef is tender.

To make the nuoc cham sauce, pound the chilli, garlic and sugar until smooth, using a pestle and mortar. Add the lime juice, vinegar, fish sauce and 4 tablespoons water and blend together well.

When the beef from the broth is tender, lift it out and slice it thinly. Add the noodles to the broth and cook gently for 2–3 minutes to soften. Add the bean sprouts, along with the sliced beef and heat for 1 minute. Strain the broth, noodles and bean sprouts to warmed serving bowls. Scatter with the beef fillet, spring onions, coriander and remaining onions or shallots. Garnish with the chillies. Serve with the nuoc cham sauce.

For tofu and flat noodle soup, replace the beef with 250 g (8 oz) tofu, cut into small squares and drained on kitchen paper. Sear as above. Replace the beef stock with the same quantity of vegetable stock (see page 190) and replace the fish sauce with the same quantity of soy sauce throughout. Reduce the cooking time to 20 minutes. Add 150 g (5 oz) frozen soya beans with the noodles.

144

oxtail stew

Serves **4**
Preparation time **20 minutes**
Cooking time **3¾ hours**

2 tablespoons **plain flour**
1 tablespoon **mustard powder**
1 teaspoon **celery salt**
2 kg (4 lb) **oxtail**
50 g (2 oz) **butter**
2 tablespoons **oil**
2 **onions**, sliced
3 **large carrots**, sliced
3 **bay leaves**
100 g (3½ oz) **tomato purée**
100 ml (3½ fl oz) **dry sherry**
1 litre (1¾ pints) **beef stock** or **vegetable stock**
   (see pages 138 and 190)
salt and pepper

Mix together the flour, mustard powder and celery salt on a large plate and use to coat the oxtail pieces. Melt half the butter with 1 tablespoon of the oil in a large, flameproof casserole. Brown the oxtail, half at a time, and drain to a plate.

Add the onions and carrots to the pan with the remaining butter and oil. Fry until beginning to brown. Return the oxtail to the pan with the bay leaves and any remaining flour left on the plate.

Mix together the tomato purée, sherry and stock and add to the dish. Bring to the boil, then reduce the heat and cover with a lid.

Place in a preheated oven, 150°C (300°F), Gas Mark 2, for about 3½ hours or until the meat is meltingly tender and falling from the bone. Check the seasoning and serve with plenty of warmed bread.

For oxtail, herb and red wine stew, add 1 parsnip cut into small chunks, with the onions and carrots in the second step. When returning the oxtail to the pan, add 1 teaspoon each finely chopped rosemary and thyme with the bay leaves. Replace the sherry with the same quantity of red wine.

pork & cabbage bake

Serves **4**
Preparation time **15 minutes**
Cooking time **40 minutes**

65 g (2½ oz) **butter**
500 g (1 lb) **pork and apple**
  sausages, skinned
1 **onion**, chopped
2 teaspoons **caraway seeds**
625 g (1¼ lb) **Savoy**
  cabbage, shredded
400 g (13 oz) **floury**
  potatoes, diced
200 ml (7 fl oz) **chicken stock**
  or **vegetable stock** (see
  pages 16 and 190)
1 tablespoon **cider vinegar**
salt and pepper

Melt half the butter in a shallow, flameproof casserole
and add the sausagemeat. Fry quickly, breaking the
meat up with a wooden spoon and stirring until browned.

Add the onion, caraway and a little seasoning and fry
for a further 5 minutes.

Stir in the cabbage and potatoes, mixing the
ingredients together thoroughly. Pour the stock
and cider vinegar over them and add a little more
seasoning. Dot with the remaining butter and cover
with a lid.

Bake in a preheated oven, 160°C (325°F), Gas Mark
3, for 30 minutes until the cabbage and potatoes are
very tender. Serve with chunks of wholegrain bread.

For chicken and cabbage bake, replace the
sausages with 400 g (13 oz) skinned and boned
chicken thighs, cut into chunks. Shallow-fry as above
in the first step. Instead of the Savoy cabbage, use
the same quantity of shredded red cabbage and
replace the cider vinegar with 1 tablespoon red wine
vinegar along with 2 tablespoons clear honey. Cook
as above.

pork & beetroot goulash

Serves **4**
Preparation time **30 minutes**
Cooking time **2½ hours**

2 tablespoons **olive oil**
450 g (14½ oz) **lean pork**,
  diced
2 **onions**, sliced
1 teaspoon **hot smoked**
  paprika
1 teaspoon **caraway seeds**
750 g (1½ lb) piece of
  smoked bacon knuckle
3 **bay leaves**
1.2 litres (2 pints) **water**
300 g (10 oz) **beetroot**, diced
300 g (10 oz) **red cabbage**,
  finely sliced
3 tablespoons **tomato purée**

Heat the oil in a large saucepan and fry the diced pork until browned. Add the onions, paprika and caraway and fry gently for a further 5 minutes until the onions are browned.

Add the piece of bacon knuckle, the bay leaves and measurement water. Bring to the boil, cover with a lid and reduce the heat to the lowest setting. Cook very gently for about 2 hours until the bacon knuckle is very tender and the meat falls easily from the bone.

Drain the knuckle to a plate and leave until cool enough to handle. Pull the meat from the bone and shred it back into the pan, discarding the skin and bone.

Add the beetroot, cabbage and tomato purée to the pan and cook gently, covered, for about 15 minutes until the beetroot and cabbage are tender. Check the seasoning and serve.

For swede and carrot mash to serve as an accompaniment, cook 500 g (1 lb) carrots in boiling water for 10 minutes. Add 1 kg (2 lb) swede, peeled and cut into chunks. Cook until tender. Drain thoroughly and return to the pan. Mash with 1 teaspoon chopped thyme and 3 tablespoons olive oil.

veal with wine & lemon

Serves **5–6**
Preparation time **20 minutes**
Cooking time **40 minutes**

2 tablespoons **olive oil**
1 kg (2 lb) **veal**, chopped
    into cubes
2 **onions**, sliced
4 **garlic cloves**, sliced
2 **baby fennel bulbs**, roughly
    chopped
300 ml (½ pint) **white wine**
300 ml (½ pint) **chicken stock**
    (see page 16)
rind of ½ **lemon**, cut into
    julienne strips (matchsticks)
4 **bay leaves**
1 tablespoon chopped **thyme**
salt and pepper

Heat the oil in a frying pan over a high heat, then fry off the meat in batches, draining to a plate with a slotted spoon.

Add the onions and garlic to the pan and cook over a medium heat until golden. Add the fennel and fry for a further 3–4 minutes or until softened.

Return the veal to the pan and add the wine, stock, lemon rind, bay leaves and thyme. Bring to the boil.

Reduce the heat and simmer, covered, for a further 20–25 minutes. Season to taste and serve.

For fragrant brown rice to serve as an accompaniment, wash 400 g (13 oz) brown basmati rice in a sieve until the water runs clear. Put crushed seeds from 4 cardamom pods, a large pinch of saffron threads, 1 cinnamon stick, ½ teaspoon cumin seeds and 2 bay leaves in a flameproof casserole and dry-fry over a medium heat for 2–3 minutes. Add 1 tablespoon olive oil, and when hot, stir in 1 chopped onion and cook for 10 minutes, stirring frequently. Add the rice, then stir in 600 ml (1 pint) water, 2 tablespoons lemon juice and salt and pepper. Bring to the boil, then cover and simmer for 15 minutes until all the water has been absorbed, adding a little more water if the mixture dries out before it is cooked. Leave to stand for a few minutes before serving.

spiced lamb with bean purée

Serves **2–3**

Preparation time **20 minutes, plus resting**

Cooking time **50 minutes**

2 large **baking potatoes**, cut into 1.5 cm (¾ inch) pieces

4 tablespoons **olive oil**

40 g (1½ oz) **breadcrumbs**

1 **garlic clove**, crushed

2 tablespoons chopped **fresh coriander**

1 teaspoon **ground coriander**

1 teaspoon **ground cumin**

1 **egg yolk**

1 **rack of lamb**, chined and trimmed

4 large **flat mushrooms**

150 g (5 oz) **frozen baby broad beans**

1 tablespoon chopped **mint**

100 ml (3½ fl oz) **white wine**

salt and pepper

Toss the potatoes with 2 tablespoons of the oil and salt and pepper in a small, sturdy roasting pan. Roast in a preheated oven, 200°C (400°F), Gas Mark 6, for 15 minutes.

Mix together the breadcrumbs, garlic, fresh coriander, spices and seasoning. Cut away any thick areas of fat from the skinned side of the lamb. Brush the lamb with the egg yolk and spoon the breadcrumb mixture over, pressing down gently with the back of the spoon. Brush the mushrooms with the remaining oil and a little seasoning.

Turn the potatoes in the pan and add the lamb, crusted-side uppermost. Return to the oven for 30 minutes. (The cutlets will still be slightly pink in the middle after this time, so cook for a little longer if you prefer them well done.) After 15 minutes of the cooking time, turn the potatoes in the oil and add the mushrooms. Return to the oven for the remaining cooking time.

Drain the meat to a board. Cover with foil and leave to rest for 15 minutes. Transfer the potatoes and mushrooms to a warmed serving dish.

Add the broad beans, mint and wine to the roasting pan and cook over a gentle heat for 5 minutes until the beans are tender. Tip into a blender or food processor and blend until smooth. Check the seasoning and spoon on to warmed serving plates. Carve the lamb into cutlets and add to the plates with the mushrooms and potatoes.

beef with walnut pesto

Serves **6**

Preparation time **20 minutes, plus resting**

Cooking time **1 hour 40 minutes**

150 g (5 oz) **walnut pieces**

2 **garlic cloves**, roughly chopped

50 g (2 oz) can **anchovies**

2 tablespoons **hot horseradish sauce**

25 g (1 oz) chopped **parsley**

2 tablespoons **olive oil**

1.5 kg (3 lb) **rolled topside** or **top rump of beef**

1 large **onion**, finely chopped

2 **celery sticks**, chopped

300 ml (½ pint) **red wine**

150 ml (¼ pint) **beef stock** (see page 138)

4 **carrots**, cut into chunky slices

300 g (10 oz) **baby turnips**

500 g (1 lb) **new potatoes**

200 g (7 oz) **French beans**

salt and pepper

chopped **parsley**, to garnish

Put the walnuts in a food processor or blender with the garlic, anchovies and their oil, horseradish, parsley, 1 tablespoon of the oil and plenty of black pepper and blend to a thick paste, scraping the mixture down from the sides of the bowl.

Untie the beef and open it out slightly. If there is already a split through the flesh, make the cut deeper so that it will take the stuffing. If it is a perfectly rounded piece of beef, make a deep cut so that you can pack in the stuffing. Once the stuffing is in place, reshape the meat into a roll. Tie with string, securing at 2.5 cm (1 inch) intervals. Pat the meat dry with kitchen paper and season with salt and pepper.

Heat the remaining oil in a flameproof casserole and fry the meat on all sides to brown. Drain to a plate.

Add the onion and celery to the pan and fry gently for 5 minutes. Return the meat to the pan and pour the wine and stock over it. Add the carrots and turnips. Bring just to the boil, cover with a lid and place in a preheated oven, 160°C (325°F), Gas Mark 3. Cook for 30 minutes.

Tuck the potatoes around the beef and sprinkle with salt. Return to the oven for a further 40 minutes until the potatoes are tender. Stir in the beans and return to the oven for 20 minutes until the beans have softened. Leave to rest for 15 minutes before carving the meat.

For beef with hazelnut pesto, omit the walnuts and use the same quantity of hazelnuts. Replace the anchovies with 4 tablespoons capers and the turnips with the same quantity of swede, cut into chunks.

lamb hotpot

Serves **4**
Preparation time **20 minutes**
Cooking time **2¼ hours**

8 **lamb chops**, about 1 kg
   (2 lb) total weight
50 g (2 oz) **butter**
1 tablespoon **oil**
2 teaspoons chopped
   rosemary
4 **garlic cloves**, sliced
2 **onions**, sliced
200 g (7 oz) **chestnut
   mushrooms**, halved
1 kg (2 lb) large **potatoes**,
   thinly sliced
450 ml (¾ pint) **lamb stock**
   (see page 140)
salt and pepper

Trim any excess fat from the lamb and season lightly on both sides with salt and pepper.

Melt half the butter with the oil in a shallow, flameproof casserole and fry off the lamb in batches until browned. Drain to a plate.

Return the lamb chops to the casserole, arranging them side by side, and sprinkle with the rosemary and garlic. Tuck the onions and mushrooms around them, then place the potatoes on top. Pour the stock over.

Cover with a lid or foil and bake in a preheated oven, 160°C (325°F), Gas Mark 3, for 1½ hours. Dot with the remaining butter, return to the oven and cook, uncovered, for a further 45 minutes or until the potato topping is crisped and browned.

For lamb and black pudding hotpot, add 200 g (7 oz) chopped black pudding to the casserole with the fried lamb chops. Use 1 tablespoon chopped thyme instead of the rosemary and flavour the stock with 2 tablespoons Worcestershire sauce.

lamb with orange & chickpeas

Serves **8**

Preparation time **25 minutes,
plus overnight soaking**

Cooking time **2½ hours**

225 g (7½ oz) **chickpeas**,
soaked in cold water
overnight

4 tablespoons **olive oil**

2 teaspoons **ground cumin**

1 teaspoon each **ground
cinnamon**, **ginger** and
turmeric

½ teaspoon **saffron threads**

1.5 kg (3 lb) **shoulder of
lamb**, trimmed of all fat and
cut into 2.5 cm (1 inch)
cubes

2 **onions**, roughly chopped

3 **garlic cloves**, finely chopped

2 **tomatoes**, skinned,
deseeded and chopped

12 **pitted black olives**, sliced

grated **rind** of **1 unwaxed
lemon**

grated **rind** of **1 unwaxed
orange**

6 tablespoons chopped **fresh
coriander**

salt and pepper

Drain the chickpeas and rinse under cold water. Put
them in a flameproof casserole or large saucepan,
cover with water and bring to the boil, then reduce
the heat and simmer, covered, for about 1–1½ hours
until tender.

Meanwhile, combine half the olive oil with the cumin,
cinnamon, ginger, turmeric and saffron in a large bowl,
plus ½ teaspoon salt and ½ teaspoon pepper. Add the
cubed lamb, toss and set aside in a cool place for 20
minutes. Wipe out the pan.

Heat the remaining oil in the pan. Fry the lamb in
batches until well browned, draining to a plate.

Add the onions to the pan and cook, stirring constantly
until browned. Stir in the garlic and the tomatoes with
250 ml (8 fl oz) water, stirring and scraping the base of
the pan. Return the lamb to the pan and add enough
water to just cover. Bring to the boil over a high heat
and skim off any surface foam. Reduce the heat,
cover and simmer for about 1 hour or until the meat
is tender.

Drain the chickpeas and reserve the cooking liquid.
Add the chickpeas with about 250 ml (8 fl oz) of the
cooking liquid to the lamb. Simmer for 30 minutes.

Stir in the olives and lemon and orange rind and
simmer for a final 30 minutes.

Mix in half the chopped coriander then serve garnished
with the remaining coriander. When cool, this dish may
be frozen in a plastic container.

pork & tomato linguine

Serves **4**
Preparation time **20 minutes**
Cooking time **40 minutes**

300 g (10 oz) **leg of pork**
2 teaspoons **mild paprika**
250 g (8 oz) **dried linguine**
5 tablespoons **olive oil**
50 g (2 oz) **chorizo**, diced
1 **red onion**, sliced
250 g (8 oz) **passata**
3 tablespoons **sun-dried
   tomato paste**
½ teaspoon **saffron threads**
750 ml (1¼ pints) **chicken
   stock** or **vegetable stock**
   (see pages 16 and 190)
50 g (2 oz) **fresh** or **frozen
   peas**
3 **garlic cloves**, crushed
4 tablespoons chopped
   parsley
finely grated **rind** of 1 **lemon**
salt and pepper

Toss the pork in the paprika and salt and pepper.
Roll up half the pasta in a tea towel. Run the tea towel
firmly over the edge of a work surface so that you hear
the pasta breaking into short lengths. Tip into a bowl
and break the remainder in the same way.

Heat 3 tablespoons of the oil in a large frying pan
and fry the pork, chorizo and onion very gently for
about 10 minutes until browned.

Stir in the passata, tomato paste, saffron and stock
and bring to the boil. Reduce the heat and cook very
gently for 15 minutes until the meat is tender.

Sprinkle in the pasta and stir well to mix. Cook gently,
stirring frequently, for 10 minutes until the pasta is
tender, adding a little water to the pan if the mixture
becomes dry before the pasta is cooked. Add the
peas and cook for a further 3 minutes.

Stir in the garlic, parsley, lemon rind and remaining oil.
Check the seasoning and serve.

For chicken and tomato linguine, omit the pork and
use 4 skinned and boned chicken thighs cut into
chunks. Toss the chicken in the paprika and salt and
pepper as in the first step. Follow the second step to
fry the chicken, replacing the chorizo with the same
quantity of smoked pork sausage. Cook as above,
using chicken stock.

pot-roasted pork with prunes

Serves **5–6**

Preparation time **20 minutes, plus resting**

Cooking time **2 hours**

1 kg (2 lb) skinned, boned and rolled **loin of pork**

25 g (1 oz) **butter**

1 tablespoon **olive oil**

3 tablespoons **mustard seeds**

2 **onions**, sliced

4 **garlic cloves**, crushed

2 **celery sticks**, sliced

1 tablespoon **plain flour**

1 tablespoon chopped **thyme**

300 ml (½ pint) **white wine**

150 g (5 oz) **pitted prunes**, halved

500 g (1 lb) small **new potatoes**, e.g. **Jersey Royals**

2 tablespoons chopped **mint**

salt and pepper

Rub the pork with salt and pepper. Melt the butter with the oil in a large, flameproof casserole and sear the pork on all sides. Drain to a plate.

Add the mustard seeds and onions and fry for about 5 minutes until beginning to colour. Stir in the garlic and celery and cook for 2 minutes. Add the flour and cook, stirring for 1 minute.

Stir in the thyme, wine and seasoning and let the mixture bubble up. Return the pork to the pan and cover with a lid. Transfer to a preheated oven, 160°C (325°F), Gas Mark 3, for 45 minutes.

Stir the prunes, potatoes and mint into the cooking juices around the pork and return to the oven for a further 1 hour until the potatoes are very tender. Leave to rest for 15 minutes before serving.

For pot-roasted pork with shallots and peaches,

use 4 shallots instead of the onions in the second step. Omit the prunes and add 2 sliced fresh peaches and 1 tablespoon clear honey for the final 20 minutes of cooking time.

salt beef with spring vegetables

Serves **6**

Preparation time **10 minutes,
plus resting**

Cooking time **2½ hours**

1.75 kg (3½ lb) piece of
salted and **rolled brisket**
or **silverside of beef**

1 **onion**

15 **whole cloves**

300 g (10 oz) **baby onions** or
shallots, peeled but left
whole

3 **bay leaves**

plenty of **thyme** and **parsley
sprigs**

½ teaspoon **ground allspice**

300 g (10 oz) small **carrots**

1 small **swede**, cut into small
chunks

500 g (1 lb) **floury potatoes**,
cut into chunks

pepper

chopped **parsley**, to garnish

Put the beef in a flameproof casserole in which it fits
quite snugly. Stud the onion with the cloves and add
to the casserole with the baby onions or shallots, bay
leaves, herbs, allspice and plenty of pepper.

Add just enough water to cover the beef and bring
slowly to the boil. Cover with a lid and place in a
preheated oven, 120°C (250°F), Gas Mark ½, for
2½ hours or until the meat is tender, adding the
carrots, swede and potatoes to the casserole after
1 hour of the cooking time. Leave to rest for 15
minutes before carving.

Drain the meat to a plate or board. Cut into thin slices
and serve on warmed plates with the vegetables.
Sprinkle with parsley and serve with a jug of the
cooking juices for pouring over.

For herb dumplings to serve as an accompaniment,
rub 50 g (2 oz) diced butter into 125 g (4 oz) self-
raising flour until the mixture resembles fine
breadcrumbs. Add 2 tablespoons finely chopped
flat leaf parsley and ½ teaspoon dried thyme; season
with salt and pepper. Mix with 1 lightly beaten egg
and add a little water to make a sticky dough. Using
a tablespoon, form into small balls and add to the
casserole once cooked. Let the casserole bubble up
on the hob, cover and cook for 15–20 minutes until
the dumplings have risen.

creamy pork & cider hotpot

Serves **4**
Preparation time **25 minutes**
Cooking time 1½ **hours**

625 g (1¼ lb) piece lean,
   boneless **leg of pork**
2 teaspoons **plain flour**
25 g (1 oz) **butter**
1 tablespoon **oil**
1 small **onion**, chopped
1 large **leek**, chopped
450 ml (¾ pint) **cider**
1 tablespoon chopped **sage**
2 tablespoons **grainy
   mustard**
100 ml (3½ fl oz) **crème
   fraîche**
2 **pears**, peeled, cored and
   thickly sliced
450 g (14½ oz) **sweet
   potatoes**, scrubbed and
   thinly sliced
2 tablespoons **chilli-infused
   oil**
salt
chopped parsley, to garnish

Cut the pork into small pieces, discarding any excess fat. Season the flour with a little salt and use to coat the meat.

Melt the butter with the oil in a shallow, flameproof casserole and gently fry the pork in batches until lightly browned, draining each batch to a plate.

Add the onion and leek to the casserole and fry gently for 5 minutes. Return the meat to the pan, along with the cider, sage and mustard. Bring just to the boil, then cover with a lid, reduce the heat and cook on the lowest setting for 30 minutes.

Stir the crème fraîche into the sauce and scatter the pear slices on top. Arrange the sweet potato slices in overlapping layers on top, putting the end pieces underneath and keeping the best slices for the top layer. Brush with the chilli oil and sprinkle with salt.

Place in a preheated oven, 160°C (325°F), Gas Mark 3, for 45 minutes or until the potatoes are tender and lightly browned. Scatter with the chopped parsley.

For creamy pork and white wine hotpot, replace the cider with the same quantity of dry white wine in the third step. Use the same quantity of ordinary potatoes as the sweet potatoes and layer on top as above in the fourth step. Increase the cooking time in the oven to about 1 hour.

mediterranean roast lamb

Serves **6**

Preparation time **20 minutes,
plus resting**

Cooking time **1 hour 20
minutes – 1 hour
40 minutes**

1 tablespoon **chopped
rosemary**

2 teaspoons **mild paprika**

1.5 kg (3 lb) **leg of lamb**

3 tablespoons **olive oil**

2 tablespoons **sun-dried
tomato paste**

2 **garlic cloves**, crushed

2 **red onions**, cut into wedges

1 **fennel bulb**, cut into
wedges

2 **red peppers**, deseeded and
cut into chunks

2 **orange** or **yellow peppers**,
deseeded and cut into
chunks

3 **courgettes**, thickly sliced

50 g (2 oz) **pine nuts**

300 ml (½ pint) **red** or **white
wine**

salt and pepper

Mix the rosemary and paprika with a little salt and rub
all over the surface of the lamb. Put in a large roasting
pan and roast in a preheated oven, 220°C (425°F),
Gas Mark 7, for 15 minutes.

Meanwhile, mix the oil with the tomato paste and
garlic. Put all the vegetables in a bowl, add the oil
mixture and toss the ingredients together until coated.

Reduce the oven temperature to 180°C (350°F),
Gas Mark 4. Tip the vegetables into the pan around
the lamb and scatter with the pine nuts and a little salt.
Return to the oven for a further 1 hour. (The lamb will
still be pink in the centre. If you prefer it well done,
cook for an extra 20 minutes, draining the vegetables
to a serving plate if they start to become too browned.)

Drain the lamb to a serving plate or board, ready
to carve. Cover with foil and leave to rest for
15 minutes. Using a slotted spoon, drain the
vegetables to a serving dish and keep warm.

Pour the wine into the roasting pan and bring to the
boil on the hob, scraping up the residue from the base.
Boil for a few minutes until slightly reduced and serve.

For fruited bulgar wheat to serve as an
accompaniment, put 375 g (12 oz) bulgar wheat into
a heatproof bowl with ¼ teaspoon each ground
cinnamon and nutmeg. Add 400 ml (14 fl oz) boiling
water or stock, cover and leave to rest in a warm
place for 20 minutes. Stir in 75 g (3 oz) each
chopped dates and seedless sultanas and serve.

stir-fried beef with vegetables

Serves **4**
Preparation time **15 minutes**
Cooking time **5 minutes**

3 tablespoons **rice wine vinegar**
4 tablespoons **clear honey**
4 tablespoons **light soy sauce**
3 tablespoons **mirin**
½ **cucumber**
1 **fennel bulb**, quartered
1 bunch **radishes**, trimmed
500 g (1 lb) **lean rump** or **sirloin steak**
1 tablespoon **cornflour**
5 tablespoons **stir-fry** or **wok oil** (see page 11)
1 **medium red chilli**, deseeded and thinly sliced
25 g (1 oz) **fresh root ginger**, chopped
1 bunch **spring onions**, thinly sliced
300 g (10 oz) **straight-to-wok noodles**
25 g (1 oz) chopped **fresh coriander**

Mix together the vinegar, honey, soy sauce and mirin in a small bowl.

Halve the cucumber lengthways and scoop out the seeds. Push the cucumber, fennel and radishes through a food processor fitted with a slicing attachment. (Alternatively, slice as thinly as possible by hand.)

Cut away any fat from the beef and slice very thinly. Dust with the cornflour.

Heat 2 tablespoons of the oil in a wok or large frying pan. Add the chilli, ginger and beef and stir-fry quickly for 1 minute. Drain to a large plate. Add the spring onions to the pan and stir-fry quickly for a further minute. Drain to the plate.

Heat a little more oil and stir-fry half the shredded vegetables for about 30 seconds. Drain to the plate. Stir-fry the remainder and drain to the plate.

Pour the remaining oil into the pan and add the noodles and coriander. Cook, stirring, for a few seconds to heat through and break up the noodles, then tip the beef and vegetables back into the pan. Add the vinegar mixture and cook for about 30 seconds until heated through. Serve immediately.

For stir-fried beef with Chinese vegetables, omit the cucumber, fennel and radishes. Thinly slice 200 g (7 oz) sugarsnap peas, 2 courgettes and 2 sweet peppers and stir-fry in 2 batches with a 200 g (8 oz) can water chestnuts, halved, as in the fifth step.

braised liver & bacon with prunes

Serves **4**
Preparation time **15 minutes**
Cooking time **1 hour**

400 g (13 oz) **lamb's liver**,
  sliced
2 teaspoons **plain flour**
8 **thin-cut smoked streaky
  bacon** rashers
16 **pitted prunes**
3 tablespoons **olive oil**
2 large **onions**, thinly sliced
750 g (1½ lb) large **potatoes**,
  sliced
450 ml (¾ pint) **lamb stock** or
  chicken stock (see pages
  140 and 16)
3 tablespoons roughly
  chopped **parsley**, to garnish
salt and pepper

Cut the liver into thick strips, removing any tubes. Season the flour with salt and pepper and use to coat the liver. Cut the bacon rashers in half and wrap a piece around each prune.

Heat half the oil in a flameproof casserole and fry the onions until lightly browned. Drain to a plate. Add the liver to the casserole and brown on both sides. Drain to the plate. Add the remaining oil to the pan with the bacon-wrapped prunes and fry on both sides until browned. Drain.

Arrange the potatoes in the casserole and put all the fried ingredients on top. Pour the stock over, season lightly and bring to the boil. Cover with a lid and transfer to a preheated oven, 180°C (350°F), Gas Mark 4, for 50 minutes until the potatoes are very tender. Serve sprinkled with the parsley.

For lamb's liver with cranberries and bacon, fry 2 thinly sliced onions and 150 g (5 oz) diced smoked back bacon for 10 minutes in 2 tablespoons oil. Set aside. Melt 25 g (1 oz) butter and fry 625 g (1¼ lb) sliced lamb's liver for 3 minutes over a high heat, turning once or twice, until browned on the outside and just pink in the centre. Add 75 g (3 oz) frozen cranberries and 2 tablespoons each cranberry sauce, red wine vinegar and water, season and cook for 2 minutes, stirring. Stir in the onions and bacon and heat through gently, stirring to combine.

maple pork with roasted roots

Serves **4**

Preparation time **20 minutes**

Cooking time **1½ hours**

12 **baby onions** or **shallots**, peeled but left whole

500 g (1 lb) small **waxy potatoes**, cubed

300 g (10 oz) **baby carrots**

300 g (10 oz) small **parsnips**, cut into wedges

3 tablespoons **olive oil**

2 **courgettes**, cut into chunky pieces

several **rosemary sprigs**

1 tablespoon **grainy mustard**

3 tablespoons **maple syrup**

4 large **pork chops**, trimmed of fat

salt and pepper

Scatter the onions or shallots, potatoes, carrots and parsnips in a large, sturdy roasting pan. Drizzle with the oil and shake the pan so that the vegetables are coated in oil. Sprinkle with salt and pepper and roast in a preheated oven, 190°C (375°F), Gas Mark 5, for 30 minutes until beginning to colour.

Add the courgettes and rosemary sprigs to the pan and toss the vegetables together. Return to the oven for a further 10 minutes.

Mix together the mustard, maple syrup and a little salt. Tuck the pork chops among the vegetables and brush with about half the maple glaze. Return to the oven for 20 minutes.

Turn the pork chops over and brush with the remaining maple glaze. Return to the oven for a further 15 minutes or until the chops are cooked through.

For honey and lemon pork, replace the carrots and parsnips with 2 large courgettes and 3 red peppers, cut into chunky wedges, and roast as above. Instead of the mustard and maple syrup, mix together 3 tablespoons clear honey, 2 tablespoons lemon juice and a 2.5 cm (1 inch) piece of fresh root ginger, grated, in the third step and use in the same way as the maple glaze.

one pot roast pork

Serves **4**

Preparation time **25 minutes**

Cooking time 1½ **hours**

4 boneless **pork steaks**, e.g. **leg** or **loin**, each about 2.5 cm (1 inch) thick

50 g (2 oz) **toasted hazelnuts**

1 **garlic clove**, crushed

3 **spring onions**, finely chopped

4 plump, ready-to-eat **dried apricots**, finely chopped

4 tablespoons **oil**

625 g (1¼ lb) **baking potatoes**, cut into small chunks

1 **red onion**, cut into wedges

1 **dessert apple**, peeled, cored and cut into wedges

2 **red chicory hearts**, cut into wedges

2 teaspoons **plain flour**

300 ml (½ pint) **medium cider**

salt and pepper

Using a sharp knife, make deep horizontal cuts in each of the pork steaks to make cavities for the stuffing. Make each pocket as large as possible without cutting the steaks in half completely.

Whizz the hazelnuts in the food processor until finely chopped. Add the garlic, spring onions, apricots and a little seasoning and blend until combined. Pack the mixture into the pork steaks and flatten with the palms of your hands. Season the steaks with salt and pepper.

Heat 1 tablespoon of the oil in a large, sturdy roasting pan and brown the pork on both sides. Drain.

Add the potatoes and onion to the roasting pan with the remaining oil and toss together until coated. Roast in a preheated oven, 200°C (400°F), Gas Mark 6, for 40 minutes until pale golden, turning once.

Add the pork to the pan and roast for 15 minutes. Add the apple and chicory wedges, brushing them with a little oil from the pan, and roast for a further 20 minutes or until the pork is cooked through. Drain the meat and vegetables to warmed serving plates.

Stir the flour into the pan juices, scraping up any residue around the edges of the pan. Gradually blend in the cider and cook, stirring, until thickened and bubbling. Season to taste and serve with the roast.

For roast pork with spicy prunes, mix 25 g (1 oz) breadcrumbs with 4 finely chopped plump prunes, 1 thin-cut streaky bacon rasher, finely chopped, 1 crushed garlic clove, 1 teaspoon grated fresh root ginger and seasoning. Use to stuff the pork and continue as above.

veal with tomatoes & capers

Serves **4**
Preparation time **20 minutes**
Cooking time **2¼ hours**

1 tablespoon **plain flour**
4 thick slices **shin of veal**
4 tablespoons **olive oil**
2 **onions**, finely chopped
2 **garlic cloves**, crushed
75 g (3 oz) **prosciutto**, torn
  into small pieces
pared **rind** of 1 **lemon**
300 ml (½ pint) **white wine**
several **thyme sprigs**
4 **tomatoes**, skinned and cut
  into wedges
2 tablespoons **capers**, rinsed
  and drained
salt and pepper

Season the flour with salt and pepper and use to coat the meat. Heat the oil in a flameproof casserole and fry the pieces of meat on all sides until browned. Drain.

Add the onions to the pan and fry gently for 5 minutes. Add the garlic, prosciutto and strips of lemon rind and cook for 1 minute. Add the wine and thyme sprigs and bring to the boil.

Return the veal to the casserole and tuck the tomatoes around. Scatter with the capers and cover with a lid. Place in a preheated oven, 160°C (325°F), Gas Mark 3, for about 2 hours until the meat is very tender. Check the seasoning and serve.

For spicy polenta with garlic to serve as an accompaniment, bring to the boil 900 ml (1½ pints) salted water in a large saucepan. Meanwhile, melt 25 g (1 oz) butter and fry 1 crushed garlic clove with pinch of dried chilli flakes for 1 minute. Remove from heat. Gradually whisk 150 g (5 oz) polenta into the boiling water, add the garlic butter and 2 tablespoons chopped, fresh mixed herbs. Stir over a low heat for 8–10 minutes until the polenta thickens. Remove from heat, beat in 25 g (1 oz) butter and 50 g (2 oz) freshly grated Parmesan cheese and season.

bean, pancetta & fontina risotto

Serves **2**
Preparation time **15 minutes**
Cooking time **30 minutes**

3 tablespoons **olive oil**
1 **onion**, finely chopped
3 **garlic cloves**, crushed
75 g (3 oz) **pancetta**,
  chopped
250 g (8 oz) **risotto rice**
½ teaspoon **dried mixed**
  herbs
900 ml (1½ pints) hot **chicken**
  stock or **vegetable stock**
  (see pages 16 and 190)
125 g (4 oz) **broad beans**,
  defrosted if frozen
75 g (3 oz) **peas**
75 g (3 oz) **fontina cheese**,
  coarsely grated
50 g (2 oz) **butter**
2 tablespoons freshly grated
  Parmesan cheese, plus
  extra shavings to garnish
1 tablespoon chopped **mint**
  leaves
6–8 **basil leaves**, shredded,
  plus extra to garnish
salt and pepper

Heat the oil in a large saucepan and fry the onion until softened. Add the garlic and pancetta to the pan and fry until the pancetta is golden brown. Add the rice and stir the grains into the onion mixture to coat in the oil.

With the pan still over a medium heat, add the dried mixed herbs and the hot stock to the rice and bring the mixture to the boil, stirring constantly. Season with salt and pepper and reduce to a simmer. Simmer for 10 minutes, stirring frequently. Add the broad beans and peas and continue to cook for a further 10 minutes.

Remove the pan from the heat and stir the fontina through the risotto. Dot the butter on top together with the Parmesan. Cover the pan with a lid and set aside for 2–3 minutes to allow the cheese and butter to melt into the risotto.

Remove the lid and add the mint and basil and gently stir the cheese, butter and herbs through the risotto. Serve immediately, garnished with basil leaves and extra shavings of Parmesan.

For tomato and mushroom risotto, fry the onion, then 250 g (8 oz) sliced mushrooms, 2 crushed garlic cloves, 1 teaspoon dried oregano and 3 large, finely chopped tomatoes over a low heat for 5 minutes. Stir in 400 g (13 oz) risotto rice, then a ladleful from 1 litre (1¾ pints) of hot stock and cook over a low heat until absorbed. Add the remaining stock a ladleful at a time, and cook for about 25 minutes until absorbed. Stir in 25 g (1 oz) butter, 40 g (1½ oz) Parmesan and season.

sausage & sweet potato hash

Serves **4**
Preparation time **15 minutes**
Cooking time **45 minutes**

3 tablespoons **olive oil**
8 **pork sausages**
3 large **red onions**, thinly
  sliced
1 teaspoon **caster sugar**
500 g (1 lb) **sweet potatoes**,
  scrubbed and cut into small
  chunks
8 **sage leaves**
2 tablespoons **balsamic
  vinegar**
salt and pepper

Heat the oil in a large frying pan or flameproof casserole and fry the sausages turning frequently, for about 10 minutes, until browned. Drain to a plate.

Add the onions and sugar to the pan and cook gently, stirring frequently, until lightly browned. Return the sausages to the pan with the sweet potatoes, sage leaves and a little seasoning.

Cover the pan with a lid or foil and cook over a very gentle heat for about 25 minutes until the potatoes are tender.

Drizzle with the vinegar and check the seasoning before serving.

For wilted watercress with garlic and nutmeg to serve as an accompaniment, heat 4 tablespoons olive oil in a large saucepan, add 1 crushed garlic clove and cook for 30–60 seconds until soft. Add 750 g (1¼ lb) watercress and stir-fry over a high heat for 1–2 minutes until wilted. Season with salt and pepper and add grated nutmeg to taste.

daube of beef

Serves **5–6**

Preparation time **20 minutes**

Cooking time **1½ hours**

1 tablespoon **plain flour**

1 kg (2 lb) **braising beef**, diced

4 tablespoons **olive oil**

100 g (3½ oz) **streaky bacon**, chopped

1 large **onion**, chopped

4 **garlic cloves**, crushed

several pared strips **orange rind**

200 g (7 oz) **carrots**, sliced

several **thyme sprigs**

300 ml (½ pint) **red wine**

300 ml (½ pint) **beef stock** (see page 138)

100 g (3½ oz) **pitted black olives**

4 tablespoons **sun-dried tomato paste**

salt and pepper

Season the flour with salt and pepper and use to coat the beef. Heat the oil in a large, flameproof casserole and fry the meat in batches until browned, draining each batch to a plate. Add the bacon and onion to the casserole and fry for 5 minutes.

Return all the meat to the casserole with the garlic, orange rind, carrots, thyme sprigs, wine and stock. Bring almost to the boil, then cover with a lid and transfer to a preheated oven, 160°C (325°F), Gas Mark 3, for 1¼ hours or until the meat is very tender.

Put the olives and sun-dried tomato paste in a blender or food processor and blend very lightly until the olives are chopped but not puréed. Stir into the casserole and return to the oven for a further 15 minutes. Check the seasoning and serve with crusty bread, beans or mashed potato.

For beef bourguignon, place the same quantity of beef overnight in a marinade of sliced onion, parsley and thyme sprigs, crumbled bay leaf, 400 ml (14 fl oz) red burgundy and 2 tablespoons each brandy and olive oil. Cook 150 g (5 oz) diced bacon in 50 g (2 oz) butter in a flameproof casserole, then 24 small pickling onions and 500 g (1 lb) button mushrooms and set aside. Remove the beef from the marinade. Brown the beef in the casserole, stir in 1 tablespoon plain flour, then the strained marinade, 300 ml (½ pint) beef stock, 1 crushed garlic clove, 1 bouquet garni and seasoning. Simmer, covered, for 2 hours. Return the bacon, pickling onions and mushrooms, cover and simmer for 30 minutes.

vegetarian

gnocchi with spinach & gorgonzola

Serves **3–4**
Preparation time **5 minutes**
Cooking time **10 minutes**

250 g (8 oz) **baby spinach**
300 ml (½ pint) **vegetable stock**
500 g (1 lb) **potato gnocchi**
150 g (5 oz) **Gorgonzola cheese**, cut into small pieces
3 tablespoons **double cream**
plenty of freshly grated **nutmeg**
pepper

Wash the spinach leaves thoroughly, if necessary. Pat them dry on kitchen paper.

Bring the stock to the boil in a large saucepan. Tip in the gnocchi and return to the boil. Cook for 2–3 minutes or until plumped up and tender.

Stir in the cheese, cream and nutmeg and heat until the cheese melts to make a creamy sauce.

Add the spinach to the pan and cook gently for 1–2 minutes, turning the spinach with the gnocchi and sauce until wilted. Pile on to serving plates and season with plenty of black pepper.

For homemade vegetable stock, heat 2 tablespoons olive oil in a large saucepan. Add 1 large chopped onion, 2 chopped carrots, 125 g (4 oz) chopped turnip or parsnip, 3 sliced celery sticks and 125 g (4 oz) sliced mushrooms and fry gently for 5 minutes. Add 2 bay leaves, several thyme and parsley sprigs, 2 chopped tomatoes, 2 teaspoons black peppercorns and the onion skin and cover with 1.8 litres (3 pints) water. Bring to the boil, then partially cover and simmer gently for 1 hour. Cool, then strain. Refrigerate for up to 2 days or freeze.

beetroot risotto

Serves **4**

Preparation time **5–10 minutes**

Cooking time **30 minutes**

1 tablespoon **olive oil**

15 g (½ oz) **butter**

1 teaspoon **crushed** or **coarsely ground coriander seeds**

4 **spring onions**, thinly sliced

400 g (13 oz) **freshly cooked beetroot**, cut into 1 cm (½ inch) dice

500 g (1 lb) **risotto rice**

1.5 litres (2½ pints) **hot vegetable stock** (see page 190)

200 g (7 oz) **cream cheese**

4 tablespoons **finely chopped dill**

salt and pepper

To garnish

dill sprigs (optional)

crème fraîche (optional)

Heat the oil and butter in a large saucepan. Add the crushed or ground coriander seeds and spring onions and stir-fry briskly for 1 minute.

Add the beetroot and the rice. Cook, stirring, for 2–3 minutes to coat all the grains with oil and butter. Gradually pour in the hot stock a ladleful at a time, stirring frequently until each ladleful is absorbed before adding the next. This should take about 25 minutes, by which time the rice should be tender, but retaining a little bite.

Stir in the cream cheese and dill and season to taste. Serve immediately, garnished with dill sprigs and a little crème fraîche, if using.

For spinach and lemon risotto, heat the oil and butter and cook 2 finely chopped shallots and 2 crushed garlic cloves for 3 minutes. Stir in 300 g (10 oz) risotto rice and gradually add 1 litre (1¾ pints) vegetable stock as above. Before you add the last of the stock, stir in 500 g (1 lb) chopped spinach, the grated rind and juice of 1 lemon and season. Increase the heat and stir, then add the remaining stock and 50 g (2 oz) butter and cook for a few minutes. Stir in 50 g (2 oz) grated Parmesan. Garnish with more Parmesan, and grated lemon rind, if you like, before serving.

goats' cheese & broad bean tortilla

Serves **4**
Preparation time **15 minutes**
Cooking time **40 minutes**

75 ml (3 fl oz) **olive oil**
1 **onion**, chopped
625 g (1¼ lb) medium-sized
  waxy potatoes, sliced
6 **eggs**
2 teaspoons **green
  peppercorns in brine**,
  rinsed, drained and lightly
  crushed
200 g (7 oz) **goats' cheese**,
  e.g. **chèvre blanc**, roughly
  crumbled
125 g (4 oz) **frozen baby
  broad beans**
salt

Heat the oil in a 24–25 cm (9½–10 inch) sturdy frying pan. Add the onion and potatoes and sprinkle with salt. Gently fry on the lowest setting for about 15–20 minutes, turning frequently, until softened. If a lot of oil is left in the pan once the potatoes are softened, drain it off, but leave a little to finish cooking.

Beat the eggs in a bowl with the green peppercorns and a little extra salt.

Toss the cheese and beans with the potato mixture until evenly combined. Spread the mixture in a thin layer and pour the eggs over the top. Reduce the heat to its lowest setting and cook gently for 10–15 minutes until almost set. Finish by cooking under a preheated moderate grill for 5 minutes until lightly browned. Serve warm or cold with a mixed salad.

For a French bean and pepper tortilla, omit the peppercorns, goats' cheese and beans and add 2 sliced red peppers, or 1 red and 1 green, and some sliced green beans with the onion and potatoes. Pour over the eggs and cook as above.

caldo verde

Serves **4**
Preparation time **15 minutes**
Cooking time **35 minutes**

125 g (4 oz) **dark green
cabbage, e.g. Cavolo Nero**
4 tablespoons **olive oil**
1 large **onion**, chopped
625 g (1½ lb) **floury
potatoes**, cut into small
chunks
2 **garlic cloves**, chopped
1 litre (1¾ pints) **vegetable
stock** (see page 190)
400 g (13 oz) can **cannellini
beans**, drained
15 g (½ oz) **fresh coriander**,
roughly chopped
salt and pepper

Discard any tough stalk ends from the cabbage and
roll the leaves up tightly. Using a large knife, shred the
cabbage as finely as possible.

Heat the oil in a large saucepan and gently fry the
onion for 5 minutes. Add the potatoes and cook,
stirring occasionally, for 10 minutes. Stir in the garlic
and cook for a further 1 minute.

Add the stock and bring to the boil. Reduce the heat
and simmer gently, covered, for about 10 minutes until
the potatoes are tender. Use a potato masher to lightly
mash the potatoes into the soup so that they are
broken up but not completely puréed.

Stir in the beans, shredded cabbage and coriander and
cook gently for a further 10 minutes. Season to taste
with salt and pepper.

For colcannon, boil 500 g (l lb) unpeeled potatoes
until tender. Drain and add 150 ml (¼ pint) milk.
Meanwhile, boil 500 g (1 lb) finely shredded green
cabbage for 10 minutes or until the cabbage is tender.
Drain and add 6 finely chopped spring onions. When
cool enough to handle, peel and mash the potatoes in
a bowl, then beat in the cabbage and spring onions.
Season and beat in 50 g (2 oz) butter.

pumpkin & root vegetable stew

Serves **8–10**
Preparation time: **20 minutes**
Cooking time: **1½–2 hours**

1 **pumpkin**, about 1.5 kg
   (3 lb)
4 tablespoons **sunflower** or
   olive oil
1 large **onion**, finely chopped
3–4 **garlic cloves**, crushed
1 small **red chilli**, deseeded
   and chopped
4 **celery sticks**, cut into
   2.5 cm (1 inch) lengths
500 g (1 lb) **carrots**, cut into
   2.5 cm (1 inch) pieces
250 g (8 oz) **parsnips**, cut
   into 2.5 cm (1 inch) pieces
2 x 400g (13 oz) cans **plum
   tomatoes**
3 tablespoons **tomato purée**
1–2 tablespoons **hot paprika**
250 ml (8 fl oz) **vegetable
   stock** (see page 190)
1 **bouquet garni**
2 x 400 g (13 oz) cans **red
   kidney beans**, drained
salt and pepper
3–4 tablespoons finely
   chopped **parsley**, to garnish

Slice the pumpkin in half across its widest part and discard the seeds and fibres. Cut the flesh into cubes, removing the skin. You should have about 1 kg (2 lb) pumpkin flesh.

Heat the oil in a large saucepan and fry the onion, garlic and chilli until soft but not coloured. Add the pumpkin and celery and fry gently for 10 minutes. Stir in the carrots, parsnips, tomatoes, tomato purée, paprika, stock and bouquet garni. Bring to the boil, then reduce the heat, cover the pan and simmer for 1–1½ hours until the vegetables are almost tender.

Add the beans and cook for 10 minutes. Season with salt and pepper and garnish with the parsley to serve. Serve with crusty bread or garlic mashed potatoes. This stew improves with reheating.

For pumpkin goulash, heat 2 tablespoons oil in a flameproof casserole and fry 1 chopped onion until soft. Stir in 1 tablespoon paprika and 1 teaspoon caraway seeds and cook for 1 minute. Add a 400 g (13 oz) can chopped tomatoes and 2 tablespoons dark muscovado sugar and bring to the boil. Add 375 g (12 oz) thickly sliced pumpkin, 250 g (8 oz) diced potatoes, a large sliced carrot and 1 chopped red pepper. Season, cover and bring to the boil, then simmer for 1–1½ hours. To serve, stir in 150 ml (¼ pint) soured cream.

tomato & bread soup

Serves **4**
Preparation time **15 minutes**
Cooking time **30 minutes**

1 kg (2 lb) **ripe vine
tomatoes**, skinned,
deseeded and chopped
300 ml (½ pint) **vegetable
stock** (see page 190)
6 tablespoons **extra-virgin
olive oil**
2 **garlic cloves**, crushed
1 teaspoon **sugar**
2 tablespoons chopped **basil**
100 g (3½ oz) day-old **bread**,
without crusts
1 tablespoon **balsamic
vinegar**
salt and pepper

Put the tomatoes in a saucepan with the stock,
2 tablespoons of the oil, the garlic, sugar and basil
and bring gradually to the boil. Cover the pan, reduce
the heat and simmer gently for 30 minutes.

Crumble the bread into the soup and stir over a low
heat until it has thickened. Stir in the vinegar and the
remaining oil and season with salt and pepper to
taste. Serve immediately or leave to cool to room
temperature.

For tomato and almond soup, bring the tomatoes,
oil, garlic and sugar to the boil as above, omitting the
basil. Reduce the heat and simmer uncovered for
15 minutes. Meanwhile, blend 150 ml (¼ pint) extra-
virgin olive oil with 15 g (½ oz) basil leaves and a
pinch of salt, until really smooth. Set aside. Stir 100 g
(3½ oz) toasted ground almonds into the soup and
serve drizzled with the basil oil.

veggie sausage hotpot

Serves **4**
Preparation time **10 minutes**
Cooking time **40 minutes**

40 g (1½ oz) **butter**, softened
1 tablespoon **olive oil**
8 **vegetarian sausages**
100 g (3½ oz) **chestnut mushrooms**, sliced
1 **red onion**, sliced
200 g (7 oz) **Puy lentils**, rinsed
400 ml (13 fl oz) **vegetable stock** (see page 190)
2 tablespoons chopped **oregano**
2 tablespoons **sun-dried tomato paste**
300 g (10 oz) **cherry tomatoes,** halved
1 **garlic clove**, crushed
2 tablespoons chopped **parsley**
8 small or 4 large slices **ciabatta**
salt and pepper

Melt half the butter with the oil in a sauté pan or flameproof casserole and fry the sausages with the mushrooms and onion until lightly browned.

Add the lentils, stock, oregano and tomato paste and mix the ingredients together. Bring to the boil and cover with a lid, then reduce the heat and cook very gently for about 20 minutes until the lentils are tender and the stock is nearly absorbed.

Stir in the tomatoes and check the seasoning. Cook for a further 5 minutes.

Meanwhile, mix the garlic and parsley with the remaining butter and spread thinly over the ciabatta slices. Arrange over the hotpot and cook under a preheated moderate grill for about 5 minutes until the bread is lightly toasted.

For spicy veggie burgers, heat 1 tablespoon oil and fry ½ red onion, 1 garlic clove and 1 teaspoon each grated ginger, ground cumin and coriander and chilli powder for 10 minutes. Cool slightly, then blend with a 400 g (13 oz) can red kidney beans, 75 g (3 oz) fresh breadcrumbs, 2 tablespoons each fresh coriander and soy sauce and salt and pepper. With wet hands, form the mixture into 8 small burgers and fry for 2–3 minutes on each side. Use the veggie burgers instead of the vegetarian sausages in the hotpot or serve them with a fresh tomato sauce.

fennel & lemon soup

Serves **4**
Preparation time **20 minutes**
Cooking time **30 minutes**

6 tablespoons **extra-virgin olive oil**
1 **onion**, chopped
250 g (8 oz) **fennel bulb**, thinly sliced
1 **potato**, diced
finely grated **rind** and **juice** of 1 **lemon**
900 ml (1½ pints) **vegetable stock** (see page 190)
salt and pepper

Black olive gremolata
1 small **garlic clove**, finely chopped
finely grated **rind** of 1 **lemon**
4 tablespoons chopped **parsley**
16 **black Greek olives**, pitted and chopped

Heat the oil in a large pan, add the onion and cook for 5–10 minutes or until beginning to soften. Add the fennel, potato and lemon rind and cook for 5 minutes until the fennel begins to soften. Pour in the stock and bring to the boil. Reduce the heat, cover the pan and simmer for about 15 minutes or until the vegetables are tender.

Meanwhile, to make the gremolata, mix together the garlic, lemon rind and parsley, then stir the chopped olives into the herb mixture. Cover and chill.

Blend the soup in a blender or food processor and pass it through a strainer to remove any strings of fennel. The soup should not be too thick, so add more stock if necessary. Return it to the rinsed pan. Taste and season well with salt, pepper and plenty of lemon juice. Pour into warmed bowls and sprinkle each serving with gremolata, to be stirred in before eating. Serve with slices of toasted crusty bread, if you like.

For green olive and thyme gremolata, mix together 1 finely chopped garlic clove, finely grated rind of 1 lemon, 4 tablespoons chopped parsley and 2 teaspoons chopped lemon thyme, then stir in 16 pitted and chopped green olives. Serve on the soup cooked as above and drizzle with lemon-infused olive oil to serve.

goats' cheese & pepper lasagne

Serves **4**

Preparation time **20 minutes, plus standing**

Cooking time **50 minutes– 1 hour**

325 g (11 oz) can or jar of **pimientos**

6 **tomatoes**, skinned and roughly chopped

1 **yellow pepper**, deseeded and finely chopped

2 **courgettes**, thinly sliced

75 g (3 oz) **sun-dried tomatoes**, thinly sliced

100 g (3½ oz) **sun-dried tomato pesto**

25 g (1 oz) **basil**

4 tablespoons **olive oil**

150 g (5 oz) **soft fresh goats' cheese**

600 ml (1 pint) **bought or homemade cheese sauce**

150 g (5 oz) **dried egg lasagne**

6 tablespoons **grated Parmesan cheese**

salt and pepper

Drain the pimientos and roughly chop. Mix in a bowl with the tomatoes, yellow pepper, courgettes, sun-dried tomatoes and pesto. Tear the basil leaves and add to the bowl with the oil and a little salt and pepper. Mix the ingredients together thoroughly.

Spoon a quarter of the ingredients into a 1.8 litre (3 pint) shallow, ovenproof dish and dot with a quarter of the goats' cheese and 4 tablespoons of the cheese sauce. Cover with a third of the lasagne sheets in a layer, breaking them to fit where necessary. Repeat the layering, finishing with a layer of the tomato mixture and goats' cheese.

Spoon the remaining cheese sauce on top and sprinkle with the Parmesan. Bake in a preheated oven, 190°C (375°F), Gas Mark 5, for 50–60 minutes until deep golden. Leave to stand for 10 minutes before serving with a leafy salad.

For homemade cheese sauce, put 500 ml (17 fl oz) milk in a saucepan with 1 small onion and 1 bay leaf. Heat until just boiling, then remove from the heat and leave to infuse for 20 minutes. Strain the milk into a jug. Melt 50 g (2 oz) butter, tip in 50 g (2 oz) plain flour and stir in quickly. Cook, stirring, for 1–2 minutes, then, off the heat, gradually whisk in the milk until blended. Bring gently to the boil, stirring, and cook for 2 minutes. Off the heat, stir in 125 g (4 oz) grated Cheddar or Gruyère.

butter bean & tomato soup

Serves **4**
Preparation time **10 minutes**
Cooking time **20 minutes**

3 tablespoons **olive oil**
1 **onion**, finely chopped
2 **celery sticks**, thinly sliced
2 **garlic cloves**, thinly sliced
2 x 400 g (13 oz) cans **butter
beans**, rinsed and drained
4 tablespoons **sun-dried
tomato paste**
900 ml (1½ pints) **vegetable
stock** (see page 190)
1 tablespoon chopped
rosemary or **thyme**
salt and pepper
Parmesan cheese shavings,
to serve

Heat the oil in a saucepan. Add the onion and fry for
3 minutes until softened. Add the celery and garlic
and fry for 2 minutes.

Add the butter beans, sun-dried tomato paste, stock,
rosemary or thyme and a little salt and pepper. Bring
to the boil, then reduce the heat, cover and simmer
gently for 15 minutes. Serve sprinkled with the
Parmesan shavings. This soup makes a light main
course served with bread and plenty of Parmesan.

For spiced carrot and lentil soup, in a saucepan,
heat 2 tablespoons oil and fry 1 chopped onion,
2 crushed garlic cloves and 375 g (12 oz) chopped
carrots for 10 minutes. Add a 400 g (13 oz) can
lentils, drained, 2 teaspoons ground coriander, 1
teaspoon ground cumin and 1 tablespoon chopped
thyme and fry for 1 minute. Stir in 1 litre (1¾ pints)
vegetable stock, a 400 g (13 oz) can chopped
tomatoes and 2 teaspoons lemon juice and bring
to the boil. Cover and simmer gently for 20 minutes.
Blend until smooth then warm through.

bean chilli with avocado salsa

Serves **4–6**
Preparation time **15 minutes**
Cooking time **30 minutes**

3 tablespoons **olive oil**
2 teaspoons **cumin seeds**,
    crushed
1 teaspoon **dried oregano**
1 **red onion**, chopped
1 **celery stick**, chopped
1 **medium-strength red chilli**,
    deseeded and sliced
2 x 400 g (13 oz) cans
    chopped tomatoes
50 g (2 oz) **sun-dried**
    tomatoes, thinly sliced
2 teaspoons **sugar**
300 ml (½ pint) **vegetable**
    stock (see page 190)
2 x 400 g (13 oz) cans **red**
    kidney beans
handful of **fresh coriander**,
    chopped
1 small **avocado**
2 **tomatoes**
2 tablespoons **sweet chilli**
    sauce
2 teaspoons **lime juice**
100 g (3 ½ oz) **soured cream**
salt and pepper

Heat the oil in a large saucepan. Add the cumin seeds, oregano, onion, celery and chilli and cook gently, stirring, for about 6–8 minutes until the vegetables start to colour.

Add the canned tomatoes, sun-dried tomatoes, sugar, stock, beans and coriander and bring to the boil. Reduce the heat and simmer for about 20 minutes until the juices are thickened and pulpy.

To make the salsa, finely dice the avocado and put it in a small bowl. Halve the tomatoes, scoop out the seeds and finely dice the flesh. Add to the bowl with the chilli sauce and lime juice. Mix well.

Season the bean mixture and spoon into bowls. Top with spoonfuls of soured cream and the avocado salsa. Serve with toasted pitta or flat breads.

For bean stew, heat 4 tablespoons olive oil in a small saucepan and gently fry 2 crushed garlic cloves, 1 tablespoon chopped rosemary and 2 teaspoons grated lemon rind for 3 minutes. Add 2 x 400 g (13 oz) cans butter beans with their liquid, 4 large skinned and chopped tomatoes and a little chilli powder. Bring to the boil, then simmer over a high heat for 8–10 minutes until the sauce is thickened. Season and serve with the avocado salsa and soured cream.

beans with coconut & cashews

Serves **4**
Preparation time **8 minutes**
Cooking time **25 minutes**

3 tablespoons **groundnut** or
   vegetable oil
2 **onions**, chopped
2 **small carrots**, thinly sliced
3 **garlic cloves**, crushed
1 **red pepper**, deseeded and
   chopped
2 **bay leaves**
1 tablespoon **paprika**
3 tablespoons **tomato purée**
400 ml (14 fl oz) can **coconut**
   milk
200 g (7 oz) can **chopped**
   tomatoes
150 ml (¼ pint) **vegetable**
   stock (see page 190)
400 g (13 oz) can **red kidney**
   beans, rinsed and drained
100 g (3½ oz) **unsalted**
   cashew nuts, toasted
small handful of **fresh**
   coriander, roughly chopped
salt and pepper

Heat the oil in a large saucepan. Add the onions and carrots and fry for 3 minutes. Add the garlic, red pepper and bay leaves and fry for 5 minutes until the vegetables are soft and well browned.

Stir in the paprika, tomato purée, coconut milk, tomatoes, stock and beans and bring to the boil. Reduce the heat and simmer, uncovered, for 15 minutes until the vegetables are tender.

Stir in the cashew nuts and coriander, season to taste with salt and pepper and heat through for 2 minutes. Serve with warmed grainy bread or boiled rice.

For red rice pilaf, to serve as an accompaniment, place 275 g (9 oz) Camargue red rice in a saucepan with 900 ml (1½ pints) hot vegetable stock and 1 crushed garlic clove. Bring to the boil, then reduce the heat and simmer gently for 20–25 minutes or until the rice is tender, adding a little water if the mixture boils dry. Stir in 2 tablespoons chopped parsley, the finely grated rind and juice of 1 lemon, 2 tablespoons olive oil and 1 teaspoon caster sugar, then season to taste with salt and pepper.

pasta in creamy vegetable broth

Serves **3–4**
Preparation time **10 minutes**
Cooking time **15 minutes**

3 tablespoons **olive oil**
1 large **fennel bulb**, finely
chopped
150 g (5 oz) **button
mushrooms**, halved
2 tablespoons chopped
tarragon, parsley or **fennel**
750 ml (1¼ pints) **vegetable
stock** (se page 190)
200 g (7 oz) **purple sprouting
broccoli**, halved lengthways
and cut into 5 cm (2 inch)
lengths
300 g (10 oz) **ready-made
cheese** or **spinach tortellini**
or **ravioli**
6 tablespoons **double cream**
plenty of **freshly grated
nutmeg**
salt and pepper
freshly grated **Parmesan
cheese**, to garnish

Heat the oil in a large saucepan. Add the fennel and cook gently, stirring frequently, for about 5 minutes until soft. Add the mushrooms and cook for a further 5 minutes.

Add the herbs and stock and bring to the boil. Tip in the broccoli and return to the boil. Add the pasta and cook for about 3 minutes until the pasta is tender.

Stir in the cream and nutmeg and season to taste. Ladle into soup bowls and serve garnished with Parmesan.

For pasta in chickpea and spinach soup, heat 2 tablespoons oil in a large saucepan and fry 2 crushed garlic cloves, 1 chopped onion and 1 tablespoon chopped rosemary for 5 minutes until soft. Add 2 x 400 g (13 oz) cans chickpeas with their liquid and 1.2 litres (2 pints) vegetable stock and bring to the boil, then cover and simmer for 30 minutes. Add 75 g (3 oz) small pasta shapes and return to the boil, then simmer for 8 minutes. Stir in 125 g (4 oz) shredded spinach and cook for 5 minutes until the pasta and spinach are tender. Season and serve topped with grated nutmeg, Parmesan and croûtons.

rösti with tomato & three cheeses

Serves **2**
Preparation time **20 minutes**
Cooking time **25 minutes**

400 g (13 oz) **waxy potatoes**
½ small **onion**, grated
1 teaspoon **dried oregano**
25 g (1 oz) **butter**
1 tablespoon **olive oil**
3 small **tomatoes**, sliced
50 g (2 oz) **Gruyère cheese**,
  grated
75 g (3 oz) **mozzarella
  cheese**, sliced
2 tablespoons freshly grated
  Parmesan cheese
handful of **pitted black olives**
salt and pepper
small **basil leaves**, to garnish

Coarsely grate the potatoes and pat dry between several sheets of kitchen paper. Mix thoroughly in a bowl with the onion, oregano and plenty of seasoning.

Melt the butter with the oil in a medium-sized, heavy-based frying pan. Tip in the rösti mixture and spread it out in an even layer, pressing down gently to compact it.

Cook over a very gentle heat for about 10 minutes or until the underside has turned golden. Test by lifting at the edge. To turn the rösti, invert it on to a plate and then slide it back into the pan to cook the base for a further 5–10 minutes until crisp and golden.

Arrange the tomato slices on top, seasoning with a little pepper. Sprinkle the Gruyère over the tomatoes and arrange the mozzarella slices on top. Sprinkle with the Parmesan and scatter with the olives.

Cook under a preheated moderate grill for about 5 minutes until the cheese bubbles and begins to colour. Garnish with basil leaves and serve with a green salad.

For rösti with mushroom and soured cream, grate 375 g (12 oz) waxy potatoes and pat dry. Combine with 1 sliced onion, 1 tablespoon chopped dill, ½ teaspoon salt and 15 g (½ oz) plain flour, then add 1 beaten egg. Heat a little oil in a nonstick pan, divide the rösti mixture into 8 and fry for 3–4 minutes on each side. Keep warm. For the sauce, melt 25 g (1 oz) butter and fry 2 chopped shallots and 1 crushed garlic clove for 5 minutes, then stir-fry 375 g (12 oz) button mushrooms for 5–6 minutes. Stir in 2 tablespoons chopped dill, 6 tablespoons soured cream and 2 teaspoons horseradish sauce, season and serve with the rösti.

green bean, miso & noodle soup

Serves **2**
Preparation time **10 minutes**
Cooking time **10 minutes**

3 tablespoons **brown miso
   paste**
1 litre (1¾ pints) **vegetable
   stock** (see page 190)
25 g (1 oz) **fresh root ginger**,
   grated
2 **garlic cloves**, thinly sliced
1 small **hot red chilli**,
   deseeded and thinly sliced
100 g (3½ oz) **soba,
   wholemeal** or **plain
   noodles**
1 bunch **spring onions**, finely
   shredded
100 g (3½ oz) **fresh** or **frozen
   peas**
250 g (8 oz) **runner beans**,
   trimmed and shredded
3 tablespoons **mirin**
1 tablespoon **sugar**
1 tablespoon **rice wine
   vinegar**

Blend the miso paste with a dash of the stock in a saucepan to make a thick, smooth paste. Add a little more stock to thin the paste and then pour in the remainder. Add the ginger, garlic and chilli and bring almost to the boil.

Reduce the heat to a gentle simmer and stir in the noodles, stirring until they have softened into the stock – about 5 minutes.

Add the spring onions, peas, runner beans, mirin, sugar and vinegar and stir well.

Cook gently for 1–2 minutes until the vegetables have softened slightly. Ladle into bowls and serve immediately.

For miso soup with tofu, make dashi stock by boiling 15 g (½ oz) kombu seaweed in 1.8 litres (3 pints) water, skimming any scum. Add 1½ tablespoons dried bonito flakes and simmer, uncovered, for 20 minutes. Off the heat, stir in ½ tablespoon dried bonito flakes and set aside for 5 minutes. Strain and return to the pan. Mix 2 tablespoons red or white miso with a little dashi stock, then add 1 tablespoon at a time to the stock, stirring until dissolved. Cut 1 small leek into fine julienne strips and 125 g (4 oz) firm tofu into small squares and add to the warm soup with 1 tablespoon wakame seaweed. Garnish with chopped chives.

chilli polenta with cherry tomatoes

Serves **4**
Preparation time **10 minutes**
Cooking time **30 minutes**

3 tablespoons **chilli-infused olive oil**
1 **garlic clove**, crushed
25 g (1 oz) **Parmesan cheese**, freshly grated
100 g (3½ oz) **sun-dried tomato pesto** (see right)
500 g (1 lb) **ready-made polenta**
250 g (8 oz) **cherry tomatoes**, halved
½ small **red onion**, thinly sliced
15 g (½ oz) chopped **parsley**
15 g (½ oz) chopped **chives**
50 g (2 oz) **black olives**, sliced
50 g (2 oz) **pine nuts**
2 tablespoons **balsamic glaze**
salt

Mix 1 tablespoon of the oil with the garlic, Parmesan and pesto. Slice the polenta horizontally into 2 thin slabs, then cut each in half to make 4 chunky slices. Cut each of the slices in half horizontally and use to sandwich the filling, making 4 sandwiches.

Arrange, slightly apart, in a shallow, ovenproof dish and bake in a preheated oven, 190°C (375°F), Gas Mark 5, for 15 minutes.

Meanwhile, mix the tomatoes in a bowl with the red onion, parsley, chives, olives, pine nuts and a little salt. Pile on top of the polenta and return to the oven for a further 15 minutes.

Beat the remaining oil with the balsamic glaze. Transfer the polenta stacks to serving plates and drizzle with the dressing. Serve with a rocket salad.

For homemade sun-dried tomato pesto, drain 125 g (4 oz) sun-dried tomatoes in oil and chop finely. Grind or process with 50 g (2 oz) pine nuts, 2 garlic cloves and 65 g (2 ½ oz) grated Parmesan. Blend to a thick paste with 125 g (4 oz) olive oil, then season. This sauce can be kept, covered and chilled, for up to 5 days.

red pepper soup

Serves **4**
Preparation time **15 minutes**
Cooking time **35 minutes**

2 **onions**, finely chopped
2 tablespoons **olive oil**
1 **garlic clove**, crushed
3 **red peppers**, deseeded
   and roughly chopped
2 **courgettes**, finely chopped
900 ml (1½ pints) **vegetable
   stock** (see page 190)
   or **water**
salt and pepper

To garnish
natural yogurt or **double
   cream**
chopped **chives**

Put the onions in a large saucepan with the oil and gently fry for 5 minutes or until softened and golden brown. Add the garlic and cook gently for 1 minute.

Add the red peppers and half the courgettes and fry for 5–8 minutes or until softened and brown.

Add the stock or water to the pan with salt and pepper and bring to the boil. Reduce the heat, cover the pan and simmer gently for 20 minutes.

When the vegetables are tender, blend the mixture in batches, to a smooth soup and return to the pan. Season to taste, reheat and serve topped with the remaining chopped courgette and garnished with yogurt or a swirl of cream and chopped chives. This vibrant and warming soup is ideal for any meal and tastes just as good warm or cold.

For Provençal peppers, heat 1 tablespoon oil and fry 2 sliced onions until soft. Add 4 sliced red peppers and 1 crushed garlic clove and cook for 5 minutes. Stir in a 400 g (13 oz) can of tomatoes, 2 tablespoons chopped fresh herbs and season. Bring to the boil, then reduce the heat and simmer, uncovered, for 15 minutes. Serve hot or cold.

balsamic braised leeks & peppers

Serves **4**
Preparation time **5 minutes**
Cooking time **20 minutes**

2 tablespoons **olive oil**
2 **leeks**, cut into 1 cm (½ inch)
  pieces
1 **orange pepper**, deseeded
  and cut into 1 cm (½ inch)
  chunks
1 **red pepper**, deseeded and
  cut into 1 cm (½ inch)
  chunks
3 tablespoons **balsamic
  vinegar**
handful of **flat leaf parsley**,
  chopped
salt and pepper

Heat the oil in a saucepan, add the leeks and orange and red peppers and stir well. Cover the pan and cook very gently for 10 minutes.

Add the balsamic vinegar and cook for a further 10 minutes without a lid. The vegetables should be brown from the vinegar and all the liquid should have evaporated.

Season well, then stir in the chopped parsley just before serving.

For balsamic braised onions, place 500 g (1 lb) peeled baby onions in a saucepan with 3 tablespoons balsamic vinegar, 3 tablespoons oilve oil, 40 g (1½ oz) light muscovado sugar, 2 tablespoons sun-dried tomato paste, several thyme spigs, a handful of sultanas and 300 ml (½ pint) water. Bring to the boil, then reduce the heat and simmer gently for about 40 minutes until the onions are tender and the sauce syrupy. Serve warm or cold.

spicy fried rice with spinach salad

Serves **3–4**
Preparation time **10 minutes**
Cooking time **10 minutes**

4 **eggs**
2 tablespoons **sherry**
2 tablespoons **light soy
  sauce**
1 bunch **spring onions**
4 tablespoons **stir-fry** or **wok
  oil** (see page 11)
75 g (3 oz) **unsalted cashew
  nuts**
1 **green pepper**, deseeded
  and finely chopped
½ teaspoon **Chinese five-
  spice powder**
250 g (8 oz) **ready-cooked
  long-grain rice**
150 g (5 oz) **baby spinach**
100 g (3½ oz) **sprouted
  mung beans** or 50 g (2 oz)
  pea shoots
salt and pepper
sweet chilli sauce, to serve

Beat the eggs with the sherry and 1 tablespoon of
the soy sauce in a small bowl. Cut 2 of the spring
onions into 7 cm (3 inch) lengths, then cut lengthways
into fine shreds. Leave in a bowl of very cold water
to curl up slightly. Finely chop the remaining spring
onions, keeping the white and green parts separate.

Heat half the oil in a large frying pan or wok and fry
the cashew nuts and green parts of the spring onions,
turning in the oil, until the cashew nuts are lightly
browned. Drain with a slotted spoon.

Add the white parts of the spring onions to the pan
and stir-fry for 1 minute. Add the beaten eggs and
cook, stirring constantly, until the egg starts to
scramble into small pieces, rather than one omelette.

Stir in the green pepper and five-spice powder with
the remaining oil and cook for 1 minute, then tip in
the cooked rice and spinach with the remaining soy
sauce, mixing the ingredients together well until
thoroughly combined and the spinach has wilted.

Return the cashew nuts and spring onions to the pan
with the mung beans or pea shoots and season to
taste. Pile on to serving plates, scatter with the drained
spring onion curls and serve with sweet chilli sauce.

For spicy fried rice with baby corn, replace the
spinach with ½ small Chinese cabbage, shredded,
and 200 g (7 oz) baby corn, sliced, and add to the
pan in the fourth step with the green pepper.

spicy bean & yogurt bake

Serves **4**
Preparation time **15 minutes**
Cooking time **1 hour**

2 teaspoons **cumin seeds**
2 teaspoons **fennel seeds**
10 **cardamom pods**
2 x 400 g (13 oz) cans **red kidney beans**, drained
4 tablespoons **olive oil**
1 **large onion**, chopped
1 **medium-strength red chilli**, deseeded and thinly sliced
finely grated **rind** of 1 **lemon**
2 **garlic cloves**, crushed
25 g (1 oz) **breadcrumbs**
100 g (3½ oz) **blanched almonds**, chopped
50 g (2 oz) **sultanas** or **raisins**, chopped
2 **eggs**
300 g (10 oz) **natural yogurt**
2 teaspoons **honey**
50 g (2 oz) **Cheddar cheese**, grated
3 **bay leaves**
salt and pepper

Crush the cumin, fennel and cardamom using a pestle and mortar. Once the cardamom pods have opened, discard the shells and lightly crush the seeds. Mix with the beans in a bowl and crush the beans lightly by mashing them against the side of the bowl with a fork.

Heat the oil in a small, 1.5 litre (2½ pint) roasting pan or flameproof casserole and gently fry the onion for 5 minutes. Add two-thirds of the chilli, reserving a few slices for a garnish, the lemon rind and the garlic and remove from the heat.

Add to the bowl with the breadcrumbs, almonds, sultanas or raisins, 1 egg and a little salt. Mix well and tip back into the pan. Spread the mixture in an even layer and pack down gently.

Beat the remaining egg in a bowl with the yogurt, honey and a little seasoning. Pour it over the bean mixture, spreading in an even layer. Scatter with the bay leaves and remaining chilli slices. Bake in a preheated oven, 160°C (325°F), Gas Mark 3, for about 50 minutes until the topping is very lightly set. Serve the bake hot.

For shredded iceberg salad to serve as an accompaniment, shred a small iceberg lettuce into a bowl and add ¼ cucumber, peeled and thinly sliced, and ½ bunch spring onions, finely chopped. Mix the grated rind and juice of 1 lime with 3 tablespoons groundnut oil and 1 tablespoon clear honey and season with salt and pepper. Toss together and serve.

green risotto

Serves **4**

Preparation time **10 minutes**

Cooking time **30 minutes**

125 g (4 oz) **butter**

1 tablespoon **olive oil**

1 **garlic clove**, crushed or chopped

1 **onion**, finely diced

300 g (10 oz) **risotto rice**

1 litre (1¾ pints) hot **vegetable stock** (see page 190)

125 g (4 oz) **green beans**, cut into short lengths

125 g (4 oz) **peas**

125 g (4 oz) **broad beans**

125 g (4 oz) **asparagus**, cut into short lengths

125 g (4 oz) **baby spinach**, chopped

75 ml (3 fl oz) **dry vermouth** or **white wine**

2 tablespoons chopped **parsley**

125 g (4 oz) **Parmesan cheese**, freshly grated

salt and pepper

Melt half the butter with the oil in a large saucepan, add the garlic and onion and fry gently for 5 minutes.

Add the rice and stir well to coat each grain with the butter and oil. Add enough stock to just cover the rice and stir well. Simmer gently, stirring frequently.

When most of the liquid is absorbed, add more stock and stir well. Continue adding the stock a little at a time, stirring until it is absorbed and the rice is tender but retaining a little bite – this will take about 25 minutes. You may not need all the stock. Add the vegetables and vermouth or wine, mix well and cook for 2 minutes.

Remove the pan from the heat, season and add the remaining butter, the parsley and the Parmesan. Mix well and serve.

For saffron and tomato risotto, omit the peas, asparagus and spinach from the above recipe. Add 75 g (3 oz) pine nuts to the pan when melting the butter. Fry until golden, then drain before adding the garlic and onions. Crumble in 1 teaspoon saffron threads with the rice. Add 300 g (10 oz) halved cherry tomatoes at the end of the third step, cooking for 2–3 minutes until heated through, then stir in the pine nuts and a handful of shredded basil leaves.

pumpkin, leek & potato bake

Serves **4**
Preparation time **30 minutes**
Cooking time **2 hours**

4 tablespoons **hot
horseradish sauce**
1 tablespoon chopped **thyme**
300 ml (½ pint) **double cream**
1 large **leek**, finely shredded
100 g (3½ oz) **walnuts**,
roughly chopped
500 g (1 lb) **pumpkin**
750 g (1½ lb) **baking
potatoes**, thinly sliced
150 ml (¼ pint) **vegetable
stock** (see page 190)
50 g (2 oz) **breadcrumbs**
40 g (1½ oz) **butter**, melted
2 tablespoons **pumpkin
seeds**
salt

Mix the horseradish sauce in a large bowl with the
thyme and half the cream. Add the leek and all but
2 tablespoons of the walnuts and mix well.

Cut the pumpkin into chunks, discarding the skin
and seeds. Thinly slice the chunks.

Scatter half the potatoes in a 2 litre (3½ pint) shallow,
ovenproof dish, seasoning lightly with salt, and cover
with half the pumpkin chunks. Spoon the leek mixture
on top, spreading in an even layer. Arrange the
remaining pumpkin slices on top and then the
remaining potato slices. Sprinkle with salt.

Mix the remaining cream with the stock and pour
over the potatoes. Mix the breadcrumbs with the
butter and sprinkle over the top. Scatter with the
pumpkin seeds and remaining nuts. Cover with foil
and bake in a preheated oven, 180°C (350°F), Gas
Mark 4, for 1 hour. Remove the foil and bake for
a further 45–60 minutes until golden and the
vegetables feel tender when pierced with a knife.

For spicy pumpkin and potato bake, use a finely
chopped chilli or 50 g (2 oz) grated fresh root ginger
instead of the horseradish. Replace the leek with
1 large bunch spring onions, finely chopped. Bake
as above until the vegetables are tender.

quick & easy miso soup

Serves **4**
Preparation time **10 minutes**
Cooking time **10 minutes**

1 quantity **vegetable stock**
  (see page 190)
2 tablespoons **miso paste**
125 g (4 oz) **shiitake
  mushrooms**, sliced
200 g (7 oz) **firm tofu**, cubed

Put the stock in a saucepan and heat until simmering.

Add the miso paste, shiitake mushrooms and tofu
to the stock and simmer gently for 5 minutes. Serve
immediately with rice.

For sticky rice, to serve as an accompaniment, wash
300 g (10 oz) glutinous rice in several changes of
water and drain. Put in a large mixing bowl, cover with
cold water and leave to soak for about 1 hour. Drain
the rice and wash it again. Put in a saucepan with
300 ml (½ pint) water and bring to a simmer. Cover
and cook very gently for 20 minutes or until the water
is absorbed and the rice is tender. Add a little more
water if the pan dries out before the rice is cooked.

index

acknowledgements

Executive Editor: Nicky Hill
Editor: Kerenza Swift
Deputy Creative Director: Karen Sawyer
Designer: Rebecca Johns, Cobalt id
Photographer: Lis Parsons
Food Stylist: Joanna Farrow
Prop Stylist: Liz Hippisley
Senior Production Controller: Manjit Sihra

Special Photography: © Octopus Publishing Group Limited/Lis Parsons
Other Photography: © Octopus Publishing Group Limited David Loftus 32, 74, 109, 144, 224, 231; Frank Adam 84, 92; Ian Wallace 19, 101, 183, 201; Lis Parsons 13, 34, 204, 235; William Lingwood 114, 122; William Reavell 12, 208.